TH[...]

GODDESS

The Goddess Hera extends her arms to welcome worshippers entering the sanctum. Fifth century BC, Tarentum, Italy: Berlin Museum.

THE YEAR OF THE
GODDESS

A Perpetual Calender of Festivals

LAWRENCE DURDIN-ROBERTSON

THE AQUARIAN PRESS

First published 1990

Illustrations from the Egyptian Tarot *deck reproduced by permission of U.S. Games Systems, Inc., Stamford, CT 06902, USA. © U.S. Games Systems, Inc. 1980.*

Cover: *Embraced by the Goddess Hathor, the Pharaoh Seti I inhales Her life-giving necklace. Nineteenth dynasty wall painting from the Tomb of Seti I, Valley of the Kings, Thebes, Egypt: Louvre, Réunion des Musées Nationaux.*

British Library Cataloguing in Publication Data

Durdin-Robertson, Lawrence
The year of the goddess.
1. Goddesses. Worship
I. Title
291, 2' 11

ISBN 0-85030-859-3

The Aquarian Press is part of the Thorsons Publishing Group, Wellingborough, Northamptonshire, NN8 2RQ, England.

Typeset by Burns & Smith, Derby.

Printed in Great Britain by Woolnough Bookbinding Limited, Irthlingborough, Northamptonshire

1 3 5 7 9 10 8 6 4 2

Contents

Introduction

This book is a perpetual calendar of the main feasts and rituals held in honour of the Great Mother of the universe under myriad names, as gathered from the earliest records of history, and perpetuated into early Christianity and village folklore.

To perceive the overall pattern that lies behind Her forms, one need look no further than the dome of the starry heavens that forms the backdrop for the revolving earth against which the changes of the year and its seasons are measured. The Goddess *is* the heavens, and She *is* the year, controlling the northward and southward paths of the sun, the two solstitial colures represented by two lions.

According to the mood of the progress of the year, so is She ap-

Figure 1   Minoan/Mycenaean seal showing the Mistress of the Beasts. 1600–1400 BC, tomb chamber, Mycenae, Greece: Athens Museum.

propriately named and mythologized. The key feasts fall at eight equal dividing points of the year, at the equinoxes and solstices (named the cross-quarter feasts by the Celts), and the quarter feasts of Samhain, Oimelc, Beltane and Lughnasadh (also known as the Witches' Greater Sabbaths). This means that the cross-quarter feasts, when first the zodiac came into being at least 5000 years ago, are marked by the ingress of the Sun into one of the *fixed* zodiacal signs of Taurus, Leo, Scorpio or Aquarius. The correlation of our present-day order of months with that arrangement is therefore made for 'The First Time', as the Ancient Egyptians would have called it. Hence there is a slippage of over a month from our present alignment of months and signs. Only in this way does the sense of what the goddesses stand for emerge.

The diagram also shows that the quarter feasts are *junctures between two months*, times at the end of one month where a period of darkness culminates in the appearance of the New Moon at the onset of the next month. It would be over-simple to state that the Sun feasts are male

Figure 2 The Year divided into the eight principal calendar feasts: drawn by Malcolm Stewart.

in nature and the Moon feasts female, for male gods such as Tammuz, Osiris or Christ were often an integral part of goddess festivals, and are without question lunar in the process of their death and resurrection, the three-day period involved being just such a join, the Neomenia, where at the end of the month before the New Year the Moon disappears altogether, reappearing after two days of darkness as the New Moon which through its light has regained contact with the rays of the Sun.

Between them, then, the eight major feasts reconcile the solar and lunar measures of a 365.25-day year versus a 354-day year, and the feasts of the Goddesses served to measure the calendar.

The reason that feasts extend over several days around one of these nodal points of the year in some cases, or that several goddesses/saints are celebrated within a short space of each other around the same juncture of the year, indicates (if the rites are put in chronological order of each civilization in history, as this book tries to do) that most are in essence marking the same major division of the year which, due to the precession of the equinoxes, has gradually slipped back in date, day by day, over the centuries. The old dates and the new, astronomically correct days have all therefore been retained, so tenacious is human nature in keeping to what was done before as well as recognizing that timing has changed. Slippages can also be explained by the use of different calendars by different civilizations — but we do not want to make this book overtechnical, beyond creating a general awareness as to why the calendar here presented is not mechanically exact in its form — there are many rough edges to the marking of time.

The calendar shows great activity and long tradition associated with the key nodal points of the year, and this book reflects such fluctuation. Some months have little activity at all, as if they are recovery periods after the climactic events of the initiations in the month before — a time to come down to earth and proceed with every-day life.

The present perpetual calendar, therefore, is more an accretion of festival points as recorded over centuries of human history, whose boundaries, due to changes in the planets' behaviour against the fixed marks of the stars, have now become extended blurs. Having realized this, the users of the calendar may feel it appropriate sometimes, in the light of any technical knowledge they may have, to shift their own worship timing to fit the hour and day of our present position in the universe, once they are tuned in to the inner nature of a particular goddess, her rite and her season. Many of the books in the bibliography give fuller information on specific calendars and feasts used in different countries, and the names of their months.

As regards what rituals to use, should the reader wish to enact them rather than simply read about them, in many cases the historical record has preserved precise accounts of rites and the wording of prayers and hymns. Some are included in the calendar, while others may be pur-

sued in the bibliography at the back of the book. What could be better, and safer, than to use the traditional practices? In many cases, those
described most fully in the Graeco-Roman world were a last survival
from the millennia-long example set in the temples of Egypt or
Mesopotamia. The continued worship of Isis at Philae as late as the
third century AD is one example.

In the West, reawakening to the age-old worship of the Magna Mater
has passed its pioneering stages. Deeper scrutiny shows She is far, far
more than an earth principle. Of course, those within the bosom of
the Catholic Church have retained worship of the Virgin Mary, but
for those who have lived with the one male principle who is the focal
authority of the three monotheistic religions of Judaism, Christianity
and Islam, there is uncertainty about how to return to Her worship:
their starting point may indeed be atheism or agnosticism caused by
the dominance of the masculine principle. The Christian saints, and
most especially the Virgin Mary herself, gain resonance when seen
against the perspective of the goddesses who preceded them. There has
been an attempt to bring out the now latent presence of the Goddess
in Islam and Judaism, those traditions which reacted most strongly
against their potent roots in Goddess worship. Yet this substratum can
be unearthed therein without loss of orthodoxy.

We have laid more emphasis on the ancient goddesses that lie behind
the monotheistic religions and Goddess worship in the pagan Celtic
world. One purpose of this book we hope is to inspire those with an
allegiance to a later tradition to breathe new life into it, knowing that
it is part of an unbroken chain of allegiance to the Mother of the
universe in Her many forms.

Many of us, however, wish to regain contact with the ancient goddesses themselves. Those who find Isis more accessible than Mary the
Mother of Christ, or that Inanna speaks to them with more power than
St Bridget, should feel no slur of 'paganism' (a disincentive term used
by the early Christians which need no longer exercise a hold over us).
The worship of the great powers of life in her female aspect have changed
only their names over the years, revealing the thoroughness and com-
prehensiveness of the universe which enfolds us, The Great Mother.
We hope this book will provide an orientation.

As the calendar is a celebration of the Divine Shakti of the West,
we have included some key priestesses as well, since they were the
vehicles for the feminine power to radiate in the world, although we
hope a further book will explore the life of the priestesses and priests
who served Her in extensive detail. We trust their example will inspire
men and women of the present time to feel it is possible to find their
way of attaching themselves to and expressing the Divine Shakti,
whatever walk of life they find themselves in — as their way of con-
tributing to the universal priesshood which is sorely depleted on
planet earth at the moment. Although in this book the Hindu tradi-

tion is not represented for reasons of space, the explanation of 'Shakti' (female energy) is best taken from the first verse of *Saundaryalaharii*, a poem in praise of the Goddess by the first Shankaraachaarya of India:

> *Shivah shaktyaa yukto yadi, bhavati shaktah prabhavitum*
> *Na cedevam, devo na khalu kushalah spanditum api*

> If the Auspicous One (Shiva) is united with His Power (Shakti), He is able to create:
> If They are not thus united, then He is not capable even of stirring.

Such is our present need of the Shakti principle to revivify our inner and outer life today: it comes into play in spiritual, mental or physical, including sexual, union.

May the calendar inspire male and female worshippers alike to approach Her mysteries, be transformed by them and share the consequent radiance to the world. (Kept for self-gratification the current soon fails.) The structure of days, weeks, months and years we are built into gives us the framework of the Goddess Herself as our guide.

The Year
and
its Divisions

[General]

The Great Mother

Not only the alternation of day and night but also the changes of the months, seasons and years are subordinated to the all-powerful will of the Great Mother... The Great Mother is goddess of time. (Neumann, *The Great Mother*, p226.)

[Egyptian]

The First Mother of Time

In ancient Egypt the passage of time was registered in the temples by the periodic fluxes of the sacred baboon, the female cynocephalus or dog-headed ape. She was the first Mother of Time in the pre-human phase of symbolism, and the prototype of the clepsydral horologue. (Grant, *The Magical Revival*, p123.)

Renpet

Renpet was the goddess of the year... As a deity of time's duration she was called 'Mistress of Eternity'. (Ions, *Egyptian Mythology*, p111.)

Isis

'You set the orb of heaven spinning around the poles, you give light to the sun, you govern the universe.. At your voice the stars move, the seasons recur.' (Apuleius, *The Golden Ass*, ch.xix.)

[Mesopotamian]

Tiamat

Tiamat's body was blown up and split in half by Marduk after his battle with her, the upper half forming the inner surface of the sky, the lower the surface of the earth. (Langdon, *The Babylonian Epic of Creation*.)

In the Creation Legend the brood of monsters which were spawned

Figure 3   Isis-Urania, Queen of the Heavens. Trump III in the Egyptian Tarot pack:
Ag Müller.

by Tiamat... possessed astrological as well as mythological attributes, and some of them at least are to be identified with Zodiacal constellations. (Budge, *Gods of Egypt II*, p314.)

The Genitrix

The duality of the genitrix which commenced in the division of earth and heaven was finally deposited in the Zodiac of the twelve signs. (Massey, *The Natural Genesis I*, p471.)

Ishtar

The whole zodiacal belt was called 'The Girdle of Ishtar'. (Harding, *Women's Mysteries*), p163.)

[Anatolian]

Artemis Ephesia, Diana of Ephesus

One of the chronological eras used by Lux Madriana dates from the founding of the temple of Artemis at Ephesus. Thus a piece by them in *Astraea* 1976 is dated 'the year 3709 after the foundation of the Temple of Artemis at Ephesus and the year 118 after the appearance of our Lady at Lourdes'. (Author)

The great Diana of the Ephesians... was, according to Pliny, a small statue of ebony, made by one Canitia, though commonly believed to have been sent down from heaven. The statue was first placed in a niche, which, as we are told, the Amazons caused to be made in the trunk of an elm. In process of time ...a most stately and magnificent temple was built near the place where the elm stood, and the statue of the goddess placed in it. This was the first temple — reckoned, as well as the second, among the Wonders of the World. (*Encyclopaedia Britannica*, 1810 edn.)

'But all the cities worship Artemis of Ephesus, and individuals hold her in honour beyond all the deities. The reason in my view is the renown of the Amazons, who traditionally dedicated the image, also the extreme antiquity of the fane. Three other things as well have contributed to her renown — the size of the temple, surpassing all buildings among men, the importance of the city of the Ephesians, and the renown of the Goddess who dwells there.' (Pausanias, *Guide to Greece* IV, xxxi, 8.)

[Greek]

Hera

At festivals at Argos in honour of Juno, ...who was patroness of that city ...the priestess, a woman of the first quality, was drawn in a chariot by white oxen. The Argives always reckoned the years from her

Figure 4   The Great Mother of the Universe, a second century Roman statue of Diana of Ephesus from the site of the Great Temple of Artemis: Ephesus Museum, Turkey.

priesteshood, as the Athenians from their archons, and the Romans from their consuls. (Lempriere, *Dictionary.*)

Ananke, Necessity; The Moirai, The Fates

'We saw the spindle of Necessity (Ananke) depending from the fastening of the sky. This spindle is the cause of all the celestial revolutions, and the ball or whorl of it is eight-fold, as there are eight concentric circles or orbits (1 Fixed Stars, 2 Saturn, 3 Jupiter, 4 Mars, 5 Venus, 6 Mercury, 7 Sun and 8 Moon) imbued with appropriate motions, and each having its peculiar Siren tone. The three Fates (Moirai) sit round and set their hands to the revolutions of the spindle as it turns on the knees of their mother Necessity, where she sits enthroned. And they sing to the Music of the Spheres, Lachesis of the past, Clotho of the present, Atropos of the future.' (Plato, *Republic* X, 616B.)

The Norns

The Three Fates of Scandinavian mythology, Past, Present and Future (Urda, Verdandi and Skuld), spin the events of human life sitting under the ash-tree Yggdrasil. (Brewer, *Dictionary.*)

Always and everywhere, Ninck writes, fate was regarded by the Germanic peoples as a feminine power. The womb of the primeval mother bears all things. The Norns hold Destiny in their hands; they spin the thread, tear it off, and determine what is to come. Something of the Norns is at work in women... more than the man, the woman is able to foresee the course of events and give such advice as will bring human action into harmony with destiny. Hence their immunity, their priestessly sanctity, as attested among the Cimbri... In the Edda, Frigg

Figure 5 A Moira tames matter through Divine Principle by asserting her authority over a serpent-legged giant. Second century BC: Pergamon Museum.

and Gefjon foresee the destinies of the world. (Neumann, *The Great Mother*, p250.)

Heimarmene

Heimarmene became one of the wives of Chronos (Sanchoniathon).

Fate came, and through measure, periods and times, the gods of the heavens [Planets and Stars], the angels, the demons, and men, were fettered, so that all should come under [Her] bond and [She] should be ruler over all. (Jonas, *The Gnostic Religion*, p205.)

[English]
The Virgin Mary

In manuscripts of the Anglo-Saxons the Solar Zodiac is [called]... The Great Zodiacal Circle and The Twelve Signs; but their descendants, our English ancestry of four or five centuries ago, knew it as The Bestiary, Our Ladye's Way, and as The Circle of the Sky. (Allen, *Star Names*.)

The Eight Great Festivals
[European]
Ariadne

Covens usually meet on the 'Sabbats', the eight great festivals of European Paganism — the Quarter days and the Cross Quarter days. The greater Sabbats are: Samhain [31st October/1st November]; Oimelc [January 31st/February 1st], the winter purification festival; Beltane [30th April/1st May]; Lughnasadh [31st July/1st August]. (Adler, *Drawing Down the Moon*, p108.)

The Lesser Sabbats were the two solstices at midsummer and midwinter, and the two equinoxes in spring and autumn. These may vary by a day or two each year, as they depend upon the Sun's apparent entry into the Zodiacal signs. [Ariadne, the Goddess as a Spider, symbolizes the eightfold division of the year — Ed.]
The equinoxes and solstices were also observed by the Druids. Their Druidic names are Alban Arthuan for the winter solstice; Alban Eilir for the spring equinox; Alban Hefin for the summer solstice; and Alban Elfed for the autumn equinox. (Valiente, *ABC of Witchcraft*, pp293 & 298.)

The fire festivals are distinctly female in nature... On Beltane, May Day, there is the choosing of an earthly May Queen to represent the Goddess... this festival reflects the transformation of the young woman-virgin aspect of the Goddess into the Mother Goddess, in the human

Figure 6   The eight great festivals of the year correspond to the ancient division of the sky into eight, represented by the eight-petalled flower or eight-legged spider. The mother of pearl and lapis lazuli flower comes from third millennium Eridu, Mesopotamia: Iraq Museum. The spider on a cylinder seal design from Fara of the same period comes also from Meso-potamia: Berlin Museum.

sphere through the mystery of sexuality...

On May morning special attention was also given to the sacred wells and springs. These Holy Wells reflect the female aspect of the Earth Forces... at these sacred places, we can see the dark mystery of the welling up of the sacred spring, with its life-giving and healing properties. These are the female organs of the Earth forces. (McLean, *Fire Festivals*, pp7 & 18.)

Says the Goddess, 'Ye shall dance, sing, feast, make music and love, all in my praise. For mine is the ecstasy of the spirit, and mine also is joy on earth... Let my worship be within the heart that rejoiceth.' (Farrar, *What Witches Do*, p91.)

The Seasons
[Greek]

The Horae

Hesiod makes them the daughters of Justice (Themis) and gives them
the individual names of Eunomia (Good Government), Dike (Right),
and Eirene (Peace). Commonly they are, however, regarded as
Goddesses who come with the changes of seasons and make flowers
and plants grow. Their names and number vary from region to region.
In Attica these names were Thallo, Karpo and perhaps Auxo, referring
to growth, flowering and ripeness of vegetation... When Hellenic religion
developed to a more unified and intellectual state, the Seasons, whether
three or four, are also called Horae. The regularity of seasons was a
favourite argument of Greek philosophers for the existence of a divine
world order. (OCD)

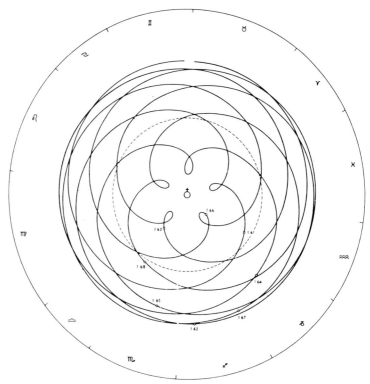

*Figure 7   Through retrograde motions on her orbit around the earth, the planet Venus
traces a five-petalled flower in the heavens, taking eight Venus years to return to the
starting point — a period of exactly five Earth years. Drawing by Joachim Schulz,
in* Movement and Rhythms of the Stars, *courtesy Floris Books.*

'Which of the individual things could equal the order that sun, moon and stars exhibit in their heavenly revolution, moving in perfectly accurate measure from eternity to eternity? And which could achieve the unfailing rule that the Horae observe, the fair ones, the begetters of all things, who in appointed order bring on day and night, summer and winter, so as to make months and years grow full?' (*De Mundo*, quoted in Jonas, *The Gnostic Religion*, p258.)

The Five-Year Cycle
[Graeco-Egyptian]

The Pentaeteris

The Pentaeteris or Lustrum which makes the space of five years, was represented by the Greeks under the Form of a Woman... Pentaeteris made a pompous Appearance in the Solemnity of Ptolemy Philadelphus, and was represented under the form of a fine woman, four Cubits high, but of an exquisite Shape; rich cloath'd, and all shining with Gold. In one Hand she carried a Crown of Leaves gather'd from the Tree call'd *Persia*; and in the other a Palm Branch. Whether these Symbols had any relation to the space of five Years, I cannot pretend to say. (Montfaucon, *Antiquities* (Supplement), p9.)

[This would be a celebration of the harmonizing effect of Venus in returning to the same point in the sky after eight of Her years, exactly fitting into five solar years — a useful bonding of solar/lunar rhythms, and the reason why Venus was set alongside the Sun and Moon in Mesopotamian arts as the third key planet. Ed.]

The Sothic Cycle
[Egyptian]

Sothis

Sirius, the Dog Star (Sothis/Isis) was, astronomically, the foundation of the entire religious system. Its celestial movements determined the Egyptian calendar which is ever known as the Sothic Calendar. Its heliacal rising marked the beginning of the Egyptian year... [This event] was so important to the ancient Egyptians that gigantic temples were constructed with their main aisles oriented precisely towards the spot on the horizon where Sirius would appear on the expected morning. The light of Sirius would be channelled along the corridor (due to the precise orientation) to flood the altar in the main sanctum as if a pin-pointed spotlight had been switched on. One such temple to the star Sirius is at Denderah. An ancient inscription from that temple informs us: 'She shines into Her temple on New Year's Day'. (Temple, *The Sirius Mystery*.)

Figure 8   The Temple of the Cow Goddess, Hathor, was originally aligned to the New Year rising of Sothis. On the ceilings of the left and right aisles in the main hall of the temple a complete rectangular zodiac is carved (see Figure 88), showing Sothis/Isis as Queen and Starting Point of The Great Computer in the sky.

The Sothic Cycle [since the year is measured by the Sun's return to the same star position of Sirius in the sky] is a period of 1460 Sothic years, or 1461 Solar Years. Thus the Sothic year is 365.25 days in contrast to the ordinary Egyptian year of 365 days. (OED/Ed)

[The five-pointed star hieroglyph] was the symbol of the star Sirius and of its presiding divine power, nothing less than that of Goddess spelt with a capital G, She of the Myriad Names who so essentially aided her wounded and beloved God to regeneration and re-establishment. She was also the Dispenser of the Unexpected. In modern terms, She grants access to the Great Computer. (Musaios, *The Lion Path*, p31.)

Figure 9   Hieroglyphs of five-pointed Sothic stars, from the fifth dynasty tomb of Kaihap, Saqqara, Egypt: British Museum.

The Calendar of Feasts
(The Great Computer)

CAPRICORN

1 January
New Year's Day
Yule — Day Seven of Twelve Days
[Mesopotamian]

Semiramis

Diodorus Siculus informs us that the word *Semiramis* in the Syrian dialect signifies 'a wild pigeon'. (*Encyclopaedia Britannica*, 1810 edn.)

Semiramis, being deified as Astarte, came to be raised to the highest honours; and her change into a dove... was evidently intended... to identify her, under the name of the Mother of the Gods, with that Divine Spirit... whose emblem, in the symbolical language of Scripture, was the Dove. (Hislop, *The Two Babylons*, p308.)

When the deified mother was represented as a Dove, what could the meaning of this representation be, but just to identify her with the Spirit of all Grace? ...Julius Firmicus says, 'The Assyrians and part of the Africans wish the *air* to have the supremacy of the elements, for they have consecrated this same under the name of Juno... Why was *air* thus identified with Juno, whose symbol was that of the third person of the Assyrian trinity? Why, but because in Chaldee the same word which signifies *air* signifies also "the Holy Ghost"'... Thus, then, the deified queen, when in all respects regarded as a veritable woman, was at the same time adored as the incarnation of the Holy Ghost, the Spirit of Peace and Love. (Hislop, *The Two Babylons*, p79.)

[Palestinian]

Ruh

The translators of the Bible have jealously crowded out of sight and suppressed every reference to the feminine form of the Deity. They... translated the feminine plural 'Elohim' by the masculine singular, 'God'.

But they have done more than this: they have carefully hidden the fact that the word *Ruach* ('Spirit') is feminine, and that consequently the Holy Ghost of the *New Testament* is a feminine potency. (Blavatsky, *The Secret Doctrine*, V, p211.)

'Spirit' — more fully also *Ruh al-Qudsh*: Holy Spirit — Mother of the Seven Planets. (Jonas, *The Gnostic Religion*, p98.)

Shekinah

She is the feminized Holy Ghost, the Presence of the Divine Peace. Venus and Isis are symbols of the Shekinah. (Regardie, *The Golden Dawn* II, p223.)

Binah

The Divine Understanding: The writings of Irenaeus, Theodoret and Epiphanius repeatedly show Simon Magus and Cerinthus making of Binah the feminine divine Spirit which inspired them. (Blavatsky, *Isis Unveiled* II, p215.)

Hokmah

The Divine Wisdom (fem.) crieth without, 'Behold, I will pour out my spirit unto you.' (*Proverbs* i, 23.)

Sephira

Sephira, or the Divine Intelligence, the mother of all the Sephiroth, is the Sophia of the refined Gnostics, of Hagion Pneuma (Holy Spirit). (Blavatsky, *Isis Unveiled*, I, p258.)

Sophia

'A knowledge of the structure of the world and the operation of the elements; the beginning and end of epochs and their middle course; the alternating solstices and the changing seasons; the cycles of the years and constellations... I learnt it all, hidden or manifest, for I was taught by Her whose skill made all things, Wisdom (Sophia).' (*The Wisdom of Solomon*, vii, 17.)

Kep, Kepha

The goddess of the seven stars [pointers to the Pole Star and Axis of the World] was the Mother of Time as Kep. (Massey, *The Natural Genesis*, II, p312.)

The Dove signified the soul or breath that was derived from the mother. The breath or spirit of life was first perceived in motherhood... This accounts for the feminine form of the creative spirit in Hebrew. (Massey, *The Natural Genesis*, I, p47.)

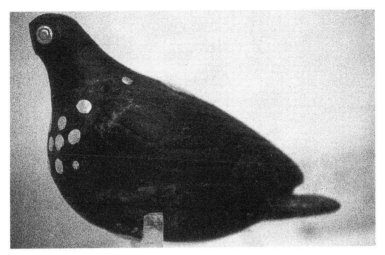

Figure 10 Votive lapis lazuli dove with gold studs in her breast from a burial c.2200 BC in ancient Susa, Mesopotamia: Louvre, Réunion des Musées Nationaux.

[Helleno-Egyptian]

'And if any accept the Gospel according to the Hebrews... [Jesus] himself saith, "Even now did my Mother the Holy Spirit take me by one of mine hairs, and carry me away unto the great mountain Thabor"' (Origen on *John ii, 12*, cited in *The Apocryphal New Testament*, p2.)

[Greek/Roman]

Hera/Juno

Kalends of January, in Roman antiquity, was a solemn festival consecrated to Juno and Janus wherein the Romans offered vows... to those deities, and exchanged presents among themselves as a token of friendship. (*Encyclopaedia Britannica*, 1810 edn.)

Gamelia

Gamelia [was] a surname of Juno, as was Gamelius of Jupiter, on account of their presiding over marriages. The Gamelia was a festival privately observed on three different occasions: the celebration of a marriage, in commemoration of a birth-day, or the anniversary of the death of a person. As it was observed generally on the first of January, marriages on that day were considered a good omen, and the month was called *Gamelion* among the Athenians. (Lempriere, *Dictionary*.)

At this time Zeus belonged to Hera and not the other way round, so he was called 'Heraios'. (Shuttle, *The Wise Wound*, 181.)

*Figure 11   Juno with her peacock. A Roman terra cotta of the first century from Tunis:
British Museum.*

Strenia

Strenae were gifts which it was customary for the Romans to make at
the New Year with accompanying good wishes. The word is connected
with the name of a Sabine tutelary goddess, Strenia, who corresponds
to the Roman Salus, and from whose precinct beside the Via Sacra
at Rome consecrated branches were carried up to the Capitoline at the
New Year. The Strenae consisted of branches of bay and palm,
sweetmeats made of honey, and figs or dates, as a good omen that the
year might bring only joy and happiness (Ovid, *Fasti*, i, 185-190). The
fruits were gilded as they are now in Germany, and the word, as well
as the custom, survives in the French *étrennes*. (Seyffert, *Dictionary*.)

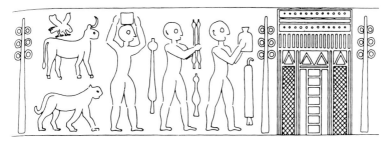

Figure 12   A procession of worshippers to Inanna's shrine at the New Year is shown on this fourth millennium cylinder seal design from Uruk, Mesopotamia: Iraq Museum.

[South American Indian]
The Goddess

On New Year's Day the Chorti Indians of Southern Guatemala drink the water from five sacred coconuts and also fertilize the ground with it. Women officiate at these ceremonies, guarding the coconuts during the night and dedicating them to the Goddess before they are drunk down on the first day of the year. (Turner, *Lady Unique* I, p49.)

2 January
Yule — Day Eight of Twelve Days
[Egyptian]

Isis

On discovering that the Ark of Osiris had been cast up by the Mediterranean in the region of Phoenician Byblos, Isis went across the sea to find it, and then shipped it back with her to Egypt. (Witt, *Isis in the Graeco-Roman World*.)

'They make an offering on the seventh day of the month Tybi, which they called "The Coming of Isis from Phoenicia."' (Plutarch, *De Iside et Osiride*, para 371D or 50.)

[Mesopotamian]

Inanna

The Nativity of Our Lady. A white candle is lit at the previous sunset to burn throughout the night and be extinguished at dawn on Nativity morning. (*Lux Madriana Calendar*.)

'We celebrate the birth of Inanna. Princess of the Earth and Queen of Heaven.' (*The Coming Age*, no.13.)

5 January
Yule — Day Eleven of Twelve Days
Eve of the Epiphany of Kore
[Graeco-Egyptian]

Kore/Persephone

In the Alexandrian Koreion the Eleusinian rite had been replaced by other ceremonies. A *drama mysticon* — in the term used by Clement of Alexandria — was performed in several acts on different levels: below the earth and upon it. Such a drama was possible in the Koreion of Alexandria... The people spent this night in the temple, singing to the accompaniment of flutes. A troupe of torchbearers entered and went down into the underground cult chamber when they brought up a statue: the wooden idol, its forehead, hands and knees adorned with golden cruciform seals, otherwise naked, was placed in a litter and carried seven times round the inner temple. (Kerenyi, *Eleusis*, p116.)

6 January
Yule — Day Twelve of Twelve Days
(Twelfth Night)
The Epiphany
[Graeco-Egyptian]

Kore/Persephone

The *Epopteia* (The Epiphany of Kore). The Beatific Vision of the Goddess perpetuates the *imitatio deae* of all *mystai*. (Kerenyi, *Eleusis*.) [In later history the pagan Feast of the Epiphany became the day of the coming of the Wise Men to view the Holy Babe — now masculine. Ed]

The Queen of Twelfth Night

A large cake was made at the festivities of Twelfth Night, usually frosted and otherwise ornamented, and with a bean or coin introduced to determine the 'king' or 'queen' of the feast. (*OED*)

A Twelfth Night Ball: Children, who came in some force... were placed within the magnetic attraction of an enormous twelfthcake which stood in a decorated recess, which was divided. The characters were drawn exclusively among the children, and the little king and queen were duly crowned, placed on a theatrical throne, and paraded in state. (Peacock, *Collected Works, Gryll Grange*, p949.)

Freya

The first Monday after January 6th was called by the Old Saxons Plough Monday, the day when men returned to the plough, or their daily work. It was customary on this day for farm labourers to draw a plough from door to door of the parish, and solicit 'plough money'. The Queen of their Banquet was Bessie, or Betsy, a caricature of Freya, the Venus of the North. The plough dragged about the village on Plough Monday was called White, because the mummers who dragged it about were dressed in white, gaudily trimmed with flowers and ribbons. (Brewer, *Dictionary*, and Whistler, *English Festivals*, p82.)

'These petitions I offer for you, ye husbandmen, and do ye offer them yourselves, and may the two goddesses grant our prayers. Long time did wars engage mankind; the sword was handier than the share; the plough ox was ousted by the charger; hoes were idle, mattocks were turned into javelins, and a helmet was made out of a heavy rake. Yoke the ox, commit the seed to the ploughed earth. Peace is the nurse of Ceres, and Ceres is the foster-child of Peace.' (Ovid, *Fasti* I, p657.)

7 January
[Egyptian]

Sekhmet

Lion-headed goddess, Time, Devourer of Time, consort of Ptah, the Bull of Memphis.
'The 12th of Tybi is the day wherein Sekhmet gave forth the Decrees' (*Sallier Papyrus*, iv). The Decrees of Sekhmet were those put forth by the Goddess at the end of the reign of Ra [at the end of the solar year and the beginning of the next — Ed]. (Maspero, *Dawn of Civilisation* p212.)

20 January
[Roman]

St Agnes

Traditionally a night for dreaming deeply and truly. If a virgin dreams tonight of a man, she sees her future husband.

Figure 13   Sekhmet, lioness consort of Ptah of Memphis, is the Measurer, and therefore the Devourer, of Time (see also Figures 90 and 91). An eighteenth dynasty icon is shown here in its original chapel in the Temple of Ptah, Karnak, Thebes, where something of her living presence is retained — so easily lost once displayed in a museum as a 'find' of archaeology.

AQUARIUS

21 January
[Phrygian]
Kybele

From his research into the archaic astronomical symbolism on classical coins, monuments, etc. Thompson concludes that the great bas-relief of the Asiatic Kybele, now in the Hermitage Museum at St Petersburg, was designed to represent the ancient axis of Aquarius and Leo. (Allan, *Star Names.*)

The Wateress with the streaming breasts is to be found in the Hermean Zodiac. (Massey, *The Natural Genesis.*)

Figure 14 The peacock of Juno, its tail suggesting the spread of the stars in the sky.

[Greek]

Hera/Juno

On a Roman zodiac Aquarius is represented by the peacock, symbol of Juno, the Greek Hera. (Allen, *Star Names*.)

The month corresponding to Aquarius was named Gamelion, the seventh month of the Attic year, from *gameo*, because it was the fashionable time for weddings. Gamelion was originally determined by the date of the new moon, and the feast of Gamelia was sacred to Hera of Weddings. (Shuttle and Redgrove, *The Wise Wound*, 181.)

31 January

Oimelc/Candlemas Eve
[Hellenic]

Hecate

(The Moon Goddess in her three-fold appearance of crescent, full and dark disc.) On the last night of the month, which was sacred to her, offerings were made to her in the crossways. (Seyffert, *Dictionary*.)

[Palestinian]

The Three Maries

In their identification of the Virgin Mary with the Triple Goddess, the Copts even ventured to combine 'the Three Maries' into a single character. (Graves, *The White Goddess*.)

[Romano-Celtic]

The Triads of Mothers

Trios of goddesses are well known in insular mythology, and although the representational form or concept is apparently the well-known mother goddess type, any one of the single goddesses invoked or portrayed in Roman Britain could appear in threefold form. This triplication is absolutely fundamental to Celtic mythology... these may be invoked either as single or triple divinities, for example, the mother goddesses whose name, *Matres* or *Matronae*, simply means 'Mothers'. (Ross, *Pagan Celtic Britain*, pp187, 207, 374.)

The High Priestess selects two women who, with herself, will represent the Triple Goddess: Maid (Enchantment), Mother (Ripeness) and Crone (Wisdom)... A Crown of Lights is prepared for the Mother and left by the altar. Traditionally the Crown should be of candles or tapers which

Figure 15 A Roman rendition of the Triple Hecate in marble, dedicated by a freed slave in the first century. She holds a sword, an ear of corn and a serpent to signify her three kingdoms of the sky, earth and underworld. Her crowns are palm-trunks which, through annual leaf growth, can still today be used to count the passing years: British Museum.

are lit during the ritual.' (Farrar, *Eight Sabbats*, p66.)

Brigantia, later Brighid

Brighid is the most widely powerful of the Celtic Goddesses. She is the power of the New Moon, of the spring of the year, and of the flowing sea. In Ireland she is most famed, and in Britain she was Goddess of the widespread tribe of the Brigantes... In Pagan times her statue was annually washed in sea or lake to celebrate her festival, being conveyed ceremonially overland in chariot or boat. In her association with a ship she may be compared to Isis (see 5 March). Always with candles and with water do we greet her, the Great Moon Mother, patroness of poetry and of all 'making' and of the arts of healing. (Denning, *Magical Philosophy*, III, p166.)

In Ireland the people prepared an image of Bride on the Eve of Brigantia, fashioned out of corn straw, and this effigy was supposed to come alive with the spirit of Bride during the night. Offerings of food and drink were also left out overnight for Bride. It was generally believed that the Saint travelled about the countryside on the Eve of her festival, bestowing her blessing on the people and on their livestock. There were various ways of indicating that her visit to house and farmyard was welcome. A very common token was the placing of a cake or pieces of bread and butter on the window-sill outside. Often a sheaf of corn was put beside the cake, as refreshment for the Saint's white cow which accompanied her on her rounds.

Over a large part of Ireland... one of the main features of St Brighid's Eve was the going about from house to house of groups of young people carrying a symbol of the Saint ('The Brideog') ... Sometimes this was a nicely dressed doll borrowed from a little girl; often such a doll was redressed or decorated for the occasion. More often the image was specially made: a sheaf of straw might be pushed into shape and suitably dressed, or garments might be stuffed with straw or hay to approximate a human figure. The foundation of the figure might be a broom or a churn-dash, or some sticks or pieces of lath fastened together, and the whole padded and dressed. The head and face might be made from a mask or a carved turnip or a piece of white cloth suitably painted or coloured. Sometimes no effigy was carried, but a chosen girl, dressed wholly or partly in white, and carrying a finely made St Brighid's cross of the local pattern, impersonated the saint. (McLean, *Four Fire Festivals*, p16.)

The Brighid Cross takes many forms, in most of which may be seen the symbolism of the Goddess. The most usual type was the diamond or lozenge of straw. The lozenge is a universal feminine emblem, and is used as such later in heraldry. The next most popular type is made by doubling rushes over each other to form an overlapping cross... a subtype of this with three legs instead of four has been noted in several

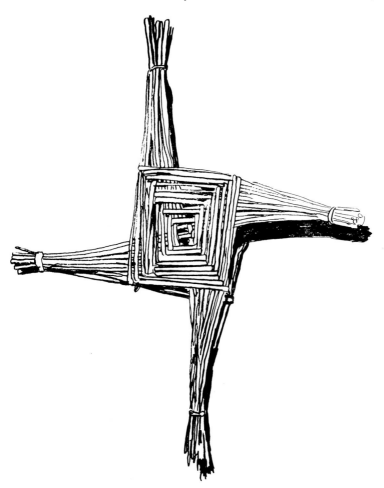

Figure 16 A St Brighid's Cross: drawn by Margaret Grant.

parts of the North. The four-legged cross has been called a swastika by some writers... The fire-wheel is particularly appropriate to Brighid, Goddess of Smithcraft, and to the later St Brighid of Kildare, keeper of The Perpetual Fire. It is also significant that Brighid's emblem is a protection against both fire and lightning.

In West Country Galway the party of young people going round on St Brighid's Eve usually carried the *crios Bride* (St Brighid's Girdle). This was a straw rope, some eight or ten feet long, spliced or woven into a loop... At each house visited the occupants were expected to pass through the *crios*, thus obtaining the protection of the saint and freedom from illness... during the coming year. (Danaher, *The Year in Ireland*.)

Figure 17   The Goddess Brigantia/St Brighid. A third century relief of the Saint
as a Celto-Roman goddess: The Royal Scottish Museum, Edinburgh, courtesy The
Trustees of the National Museums of Scotland.

For the purpose of regeneration it is directed to make an image of the female power of nature, in the shape either of a woman or of a cow. In this statue the person to be regenerated is inclosed, and dragged out through the usual channel. As a statue of pure gold and of proper dimensions would be too expensive, it is sufficient to make an image of the sacred *Yoni*, through which the person to be regenerated is to pass. (Wilford, cited by O'Brien, *Round Towers of Ireland*.)

'On the Louth-Armagh border I have heard of "Brigid's Shield" and "Brigid's Crown", and was informed of a tradition that in days gone by, the most modest and most beautiful girl of a particular area, wearing a crown of rushes, a shield on her left arm, and a cross in her right hand, was escorted by a group of young girls from house to house on Brigid's Eve or Brigid's Morning.' (T.G.F. Paterson, *Ulster Journal of Archaeology*, 1945, p46.)

1 February
The Lesser Eleusinian Mysteries — Day One of Three Days
Oimelc/Candlemas
[Greek]
Demeter and Kore/Persephone

The Lesser Eleusinian Mysteries celebrated the return of Persephone to her mother Demeter after her descent into the World on the Other Side where she was the wife of Pluto, its King.

These lesser mysteries were observed at Agrae near Ilissus... In later times the smaller festivals were preparatory to the greater, and no person could be initiated at Eleusis without a previous purification at Agrae. (Lempriere, *Dictionary*.)

The person who was to be initiated in the Lesser Mysteries, as well as the Greater, according to the original instructions was to be a person of unblemished moral character. (*Encyclopaedia Britannica*, 1810 edn.)

The Goddess, turned outwards, is seated in front of The Secrets. She is sitting on a great round basket, the *cista mystica*, in which the paraphernalia of the *myesis* are hidden. Now that the initiand is cleansed and ready, they may be shown him/her. Now he or she may receive instruction and learn what has to be learnt. Behind her mother's back She, too, stands there, the well-known figure of the Kore... *Myesis* can be rendered by the Latin word *initia* (beginnings), or its derivative *initiatio*, or initiation, signifying 'introduction into the secret'. (Kereny, *Eleusis*, pp46, 58.)

Figure 18   The Cista Mystica on a Greek coin from Pergamon: courtesy The Trustees of the British Museum.

[Romano-Celtic]
Brigantia/Brighid

St Brighid, Virgin, Patroness Saint of Ireland. In Irish folk tradition St Brighid's Day is the first day of Spring, and thus of the farmer's year. It is the festival of Ireland's venerated and much-loved saint, who is also the patroness of cattle and dairy work. (Danaher, *The Year in Ireland*, p13.)

Oi-melg (ewe-milk) is so named because this is the time the ewe's milk starts to flow. That *Oimelc* is 1 February we know from Peter O'Connell's Dictionary, where *Oimelc* is identified with *Feil Brighde* (St Brighid's Feast Day), which has been, and is still, the Irish name for 1 February throughout Ireland.

We find here the female mystery of germination of the seed, the process which spiritually was beginning to happen in the earth after the cold contractive forces of winter. Perhaps one of the most important and archetypal aspects of this festival was the lighting of candles or torches at midnight. This activity was transferred in more recent centuries to February the 2nd... At her shrine in Kildare, a sacred flame burnt continuously. (McLean, *Four Fire Festivals*, p16.)

That this custom had a pagan origin is unquestionable... 'Perhaps', writes Sir James Ware, 'it might seem to have taken its origin from an imitation of the Vestal Virgins.' (Brewer, *The Beauties of Ireland*, p30.)

In the Highlands of Scotland... the festival... was strictly matriarchal - the door of the feasting place was barred to the men of the community who had to plead humbly to honour Bride. (McLean, *Four Fire Festivals*, p17.)

In the north of England... Candlemass used to be called The Wives' Feast Day because it was regarded as a fertility festival... On February the first, as today in the Catholic Church at the Festival of Candlemass, the new fire was kindled and blessed. (Harding, *Woman's Mysteries*, pp130-1.)

Just as Hallowe'en marks the retreat into winter darkness and symbolizes menstruation at the dark of the moon, so Candlemass marks the opening out of the natural world, ovulation, and emergence into the pure light of Spring as first glimpsed at the Winter Solstice. The festivals symbolize on another level the Celtic belief in reincarnation: death at Hallowe'en followed by gestation in the dark space-womb of the Goddess and rebirth in a new body at Candlemass. This is the time for initiations... a rebirth of the spirit. (Morgan, *Matriarchy News* No.2.)

The straw or rushes left over from the making of the crosses, or from the sheaf or bundle left at the door for the saint or from 'Brighid's bed', was believed to have curative powers. Strands from it were preserved and tied about an aching head or a sore limb during the night. Others put a wisp under the mattress or pillow to ward off disease. In parts of Donegal the fishermen wore a little ribbon from the residual rushes or straw and carried it when at sea.

In a few places in County Leitrim, children... got a small piece of a flat wooden board and with the viscous exudation of a partly boiled or roasted potato fixed peeled rushes upon it in figures representing the sun, the moon and the stars — this was then hung up with the cross. (Co. *Kildare Archaeological Journal*, V, p441.)

[Romano-British]

Sul-Minerva

Sul-Minerva of Bath seems to be identical with Brighid; a goddess of knowledge and healing with an 'ashless fire' in her sanctuary. If Sul, whose name derives from the Celtic words for the eye (suil) and seeing, is cognate with the Goddess of Silbury Hill, there could well have been a procession at Candlemass to her sacred spring, the Swallowhead (Suilohead), which begins to flow again in February, when the Queen 'comes from the mound'. (Morgan, *Matriarchy News* No.2.)

2 February
Lesser Eleusinian Mysteries — Day Two
of Three Days
[Greek/Roman]
Juno Februa, The Purifier

It was the old Roman custom of burning candles to the goddess Februa, mother of Mars, to scare away evil spirits. (Brewer, *Dictionary*.)

Figure 19   A seventh century BC Corinthian version of Demeter and Kore in painted clay from Thebes, Greece: British Museum.

The Virgin Mary

The list of festivals for the whole Christian church was swelled by the consecration of the Day of the Holy Virgin Mary, that the people might not miss their *Lupercalia*, which they were accustomed to celebrate in the month of February. This was instituted in the reign of Justinian, and fixed to the second of February... The Latins called it Candlemass, because many candles were then lighted up; as had been done on the Lupercalia, the festival of Proserpine, whom her mother Ceres sought with candles. (Mosheim, *Ecclesiastical History*, II, p51 with notes by Soames.)

5 February
[Roman]

St Agatha

At Catania in Sicily remarkable resemblances have been detected between the local Feast of St Agatha, and the Isis Festival of Navigium Isidis [celebrated in earlier centuries in Egypt on 5 March] — the Saint's victorious Veil being received to the sound of tambourines such as would have pleased Isis' ear. (Ciaceri, *Culti e Miti*, p268.)

11 February
[French]

Our Lady of Lourdes

Between 11 February and 16 July 1858, Bernadette Soubirous had sixteen visions of Mary, calling herself 'Immaculate Conception', in the Grotto at Lourdes, on the spot where the marble statue is worshipped by the hopeful today.

Where a succession of cults has obtained, the same places have often been holy to each in turn. Sometimes the new manifestation takes on distinctive features which link it strangely to a former one. The cave at Lourdes, for example, which was the site of Bernadette's uniquely remarkable series of visions, had in previous centuries been a shrine of the goddess-cult. It is known that the herb which grew in the cave, and of which she ate in the course of her guided actions, was a sacred plant in the bygone cult. (Denning, *The Magical Philosophy* III, p147.)

Demeter and Persephone/The Virgin Mary

Studying the Eleusinian mysteries of Demeter and Persephone, to me the visions of Lourdes and Fatima are a portrayal of these dramas in actual human history. The Lesser Mystery was shown at Lourdes in the form of a beautiful maiden appearing in a grotto. The young girl who witnessed the visions drew forth a stream of healing water from the mud... The Lesser Mystery of Lourdes, therefore, portrayed Persephone, Queen of Day and Night... in control of the elements of Earth and Water. (Robertson, *The Call of Isis*, p125.)

In Early Christian Art, Christ as Jupiter-Pluto, and Mary as Proserpina, receive the souls that Mercury, wearing the broad-brimmed hat and carrying in his hand the rod of the soul-guide, brings to them, in the presence of the Three Fates. (Blavatsky, *Isis Unveiled*), p335.)

The Great Mother

There has been an increasing number of reports concerning the appearance of a Great Mother image which, depending upon the witnesses, has been interpreted as the Virgin Mary, Pallas Athena, Isis, Diana, or, simply, the Blessed Mother.

'It is already time that each one of us accomplishes holy deeds of his own initiative and reforms his life according to Our Lady's appeal... she told me that when other means are exhausted and despised by men, She is giving us that last anchor of salvation, that is, the Holy Virgin in Person' (Lucy, about Our Lady of Fatima). (Steiger, *Gods of Aquarius*, pp 63, 67.)

14 February
[English]

St Valentine

Like the candles of Candlemas, recently gone by, it comes to us by direct descent from the Lupercalia of pagan Rome. It was about the middle of the month that the names of willing young ladies were put in a box and well shaken up, so that each young blood could draw out one at random, the girl thus won to remain his companion while the gaieties lasted... Centuries passed and still the lottery for girls continued... 'It is a ceremony never omitted among the Vulgar', wrote Bourne in 1725, 'to draw lots which they term Valentines. The names of a select number of one sex are by an equal number of the other put into some vessel; and after that, everyone draws a name, which for the present is called their Valentine, and is also look'd upon as a good omen of their being man and wife afterwards.' (Whistler, *English Festivals*, p90.)

15 February
[Roman]

Lupa, The She-Wolf

The festival of the Lupercalia was first instituted by the Romans in honour of the she-wolf which suckled Romulus and Remus. (Lempriere, *Dictionary*.)

A she-wolf which had given birth to her whelps came, wondrous to tell, to the abandoned twins... She halted and fawned on the tender babes with her tail, and licked into shape their two bodies with her tongue... fearless, they sucked her dugs and were fed on a supply of milk that was never meant for them. The she-wolf (*lupa*) gave her name to the place, and the place gave their name to the Luperci. Great is the reward of the nurse for the milk she gave. (Ovid, *Fasti* II, 413.)

18 February
[Persian]
Spenta Armaiti

A festival of women and of cultivation celebrated by the Zoroastrians. (Duchesne-Guillemin, *Religion de l'Iran Ancien*, p119.)

PISCES

21 February
[Babylonian]

Anunit

Anunitu, 'the heavenly one' was to the Babylonians one half of our present sign, a goddess with one fish between her legs and one across her breasts. She was the patroness of Nineveh, whose name they wrote with a composite sign meaning 'house of the fish'. (Eisler, *Royal Art of Astrology*, p107.)

Figure 20 An Elamite bronze statuette of the Fish Goddess, whose skirt flounces rhyme with the divisions of her tail. From Tang-i-Sarvak, Iran, c. eighteenth century BC: British Museum.

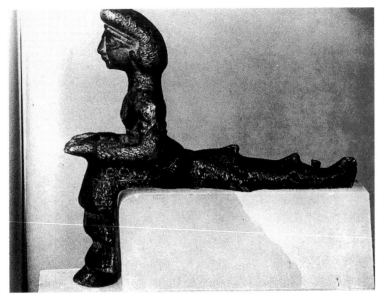

[Syrian]

Atargatis/Derceto

Al Biruni asserted that the name of the sign in all languages signifies only one fish, and it is probable that the original asterism was such, for according to Eratosthenes it symbolized the great Syrian goddess, Derketo, later named Dea Syria. The Greeks called her Atargatis, and from a supposed derivation of this word from Adir and Dag (Great and Fish) it was drawn with a woman's head upon a huge fish body. (Allen, *Star Names*.)

26 February

[Egyptian]

Mut

The powerfully protecting, primordial Vulture Goddess of Upper Egypt, later in her lioness form the wife of the God Amun of Karnak, whose joint child is the young Moon-god, Khonsu.

Every High-Priestess Queen of Egypt wore the Vulture Goddess Mut

Figure 21   Ahmose, foundress of the Eighteenth Dynasty of Egypt and mother of Queen Hatshepsut, wearing the royal high priestess Vulture head-dress of Mut, on a limestone relief fragment from the Temple of Hatshepsut at Deir-el-Bahari, Thebes, Egypt: Norfolk Museums Service (Norwich Castle Museum).

as a head-dress to signify her spiritual development, the expansion of her brain, the opening of the third eye, and the blending of her head with the Goddess of Life and Death Herself.

29 February

Leap Year Day

St Patrick, having driven the frogs out of the bogs, was walking along the shores of Lough Neagh, when he was accosted by St Brighid... and was told that a mutiny had broken out in the nunnery... the ladies claiming the right of 'popping the question'. St Patrick said he would concede them the right every seventh year, when St Brighid threw her arms round his neck and exclaimed, 'Arrah, Pathrick, jewel, I daurn't go back to the girls wid such a proposal. Make it one year in four.' St Patrick replied, 'Brighid, acushla, squeeze me that way again, an' I'll give ye leap-year, the longest of the lot.' St Brighid, upon this, popped the question to St Patrick himself. (Brewer, *Dictionary*.)

An Act of Parliament, passed in the year 1228, has been unearthed which runs thus: 'Ordonit that during ye reign of her maist blessed maistie, Margaret, ilka maiden, ladee of baith high and lowe estait, shall hae libertie to speak ye man she likes. Gif he refuses to tak hir to be his wyf, he shale be mulct in the sum of ane hundrity pundes, or less, as his estait may bee, except and alwais gif he can make it appeare that he is betrothit to anither woman, then he schall be free.' (Brewer, *Dictionary*.)

1 March

[Roman]

Juno Lucina, The Matronalia

A festival celebrated by Roman matrons on the lst of March, the anniversary of the foundation of the temple of Juno Lucina on the Esquiline. In the houses, prayers were offered for a prosperous wedlock, the women received presents from the men and waited on the slaves, just as the men did at the Saturnalia. In the temple of the Goddess, women and girls prayed to her... and brought pious offerings... At this festival Juno was represented veiled, with a flower in her right hand and an infant in swaddling clothes in her left. (Seyffert, *Dictionary*.)

Vesta

'If you would convince yourself that the Kalends of March were really the beginning of the year, you may refer to the following proofs... the withered laurel is withdrawn from the Ilian (i.e. Vestal) hearth, that Vesta also may make a brave show, dressed in fresh leaves. Besides, 'tis said that a new fire is lighted in her secret shrine, and the rekindled flame gains strength.' (Ovid, *Fasti*, III, 135.)

On every 1st March the Vestal Fire was rekindled... only by a burning glass, or by the primitive method of friction by boring a piece of wood from a fruit tree. (Seyffert, *Dictionary*.)

5 March
[Helleno-Egyptian]

Isis

The festival of The Ship of Isis (Ploiaphesia/Isidis Navigium) is held in recognition of her being the patroness of navigation and inventress of the sail. (Seyffert, *Dictionary*.)

We may mention especially the naval car (*currus navalis*) which had been inherited from pagan times...[from which the world 'carnival' is derived, and all the 'floats' on cars in such processions]. (Burckhardt, *Civilisation of the Renaissance*, p216.)

Isis addresses, Apuleius in Corinth: ' "The eternal laws of religion devote to my worship the day born of this night. Tomorrow my priests offer

Figure 22   A seal design from Kish, Mesopotamia, shows the Goddess in her festival boat: Ashmolean Museum, Oxford.

me the first-fruits of the new sailing season by dedicating a ship to me; for at this season the storms of winter lose their force, the leaping waves subside, and the sea becomes navigable once more".

'Soon a golden sun arose... and at once the streets were filled with people walking along as if in a religious triumph. Not only I, but the whole world, seemed filled with delight. The animals, the houses, even the weather itself reflected the universal joy and serenity... and the song birds, assured that spring had come, were chirping their welcome to the Queen of the Stars, the Mother of the Season, the Mistress of the Universe.

'Presently the vanguard of the grand procession came in view. It was composed of a number of people in fancy dress of their own choosing... a pretended magistrate with purple robe and rods of office; a philosopher... a tame she-bear, dressed like a woman, carried in a sedan chair; and an ape in a straw hat and saffron-coloured Phrygian cloak. These fancy-dress comedians kept running in and out of the crowd — and behind them came the procession proper.

'At the head walked women crowned with flowers, who pulled more flowers out of the folds of their beautiful dresses and scattered them along the road; their joy in the Saviouress appeared in every gesture. Next came women with polished mirrors tied to the back of their heads, which gave all who followed them the illusion of coming to meet the Goddess, rather than marching before her. Next, a party of women with ivory combs in their hands who made a pantomime of combing the Goddess's royal hair, and another party with bottles of perfume who sprinkled the road with balsam and other precious perfumes; and behind these a mixed company of women and men who... propitiated her by carrying every sort of light — lamps, torches, wax-candles and so forth.

'Next came musicians with pipes and flutes, followed by a party of carefully chosen choir-boys singing a hymn... also a number of beadles and whifflers crying: "Make way there, way for the Goddess!" Then followed a great crowd of the Goddess's initiates, men and women of all classes and every age, their pure white linen clothes shining brightly. The women wore their hair tied up in glossy coils under gauze headdresses; the men's heads were completely shaven...

'The leading priests... carried the oracular emblems of the deity. The Chief Priest held a bright lamp... it was a golden boat-shaped affair with a tall tongue of flame mounting from a hole in the centre. The second priest held an auxiliaria, or ritual pot, in each of his hands — the name refers to the Goddess's providence in helping Her devotees. The third carried a miniature palm-tree... The fourth carried a model of the left hand with the fingers stretched out, which is an emblem of justice: he also held a golden vessel rounded in the shape of a woman's breast, from the nipple of which a thin stream of milk fell to the ground. The fifth carried a winnowing-fan woven with golden rods, not osiers. Then

Figure 23   The Hand of the Goddess still abounds in the Islamic world, notably in North Africa, and is called The Hand of Fatima (the daughter of the Prophet Muhammad).

came a man, not one of the five, carrying a wine-jar.

'Next in the procession followed those deities that deigned to walk on human feet... Anubis with a face black on one side, golden on the other, walking erect... Behind danced a man carrying on his shoulders, seated upright, the statue of a cow, representing the Goddess as the fruitful Mother of us all. Then came along a priest with a box containing the secret implements of her wonderful cult. Another fortunate priest had another emblem of her godhead hidden in the lap of his robe... It was a symbol of the sublime and ineffable mysteries of the Goddess... a small vessel of burnished gold, upon which Egyptian hieroglyphics were thickly crowded, with a rounded bottom, a long spout, and a generously curving handle along which sprawled an asp raising its head and displaying its scaly, wrinkled, puffed-out throat.

'Meanwhile the pageant moved slowly on and we reached the sea-shore... There the divine emblems were arranged in due order and there with solemn prayers the chaste-lipped priest hallowed and dedicated to the Goddess a beautifully built ship, with Egyptian hieroglyphics painted over the entire hull — but first he carefully purified it with a lighted torch, an egg and sulphur. The sail was shining white linen, inscribed in large letters with a prayer for the Goddess's protection of shipping during the new sailing season. The long fir mast with its shining head was not stepped, and we admired the gilded prow shaped like the neck of Isis's holy goose, and the long brightly-polished keel cut

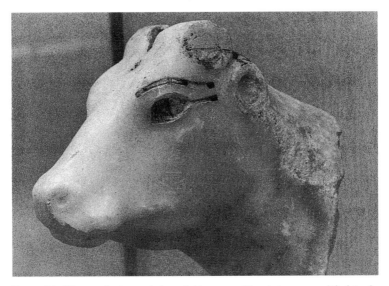

Figure 24   The comforting and dependable cow goddess is best exemplified in the Egyptian goddess, Hathor. Even this fragmentary alabaster head from the temple of Queen Hatshepsut, Deir-el-Bahari, Thebes, Egypt, retains its maternal softness: British Museum.

from a solid trunk of citrus-wood. Then all present, both priesthood and laity, began zealously stowing aboard winnowing-fans heaped with aromatics and other votive offerings and poured an abundant stream of milk into the sea as a libation. When the ship was loaded with generous gifts and prayers for good fortune, they cut the anchor cables and she slipped across the bay with a serene breeze behind her that seemed to have sprung up for her sake alone. When she stood so far out to sea that we could no longer keep her in view, the priests took up the holy emblems and started happily back towards the temple, in the same orderly procession as before.

'On our arrival the Chief Priest and the priests who carried the oracular emblems were admitted into the Goddess's adytum with other initiates and restored them to their proper places. Then one of them, known as the Doctor of Divinity... went up into a high pulpit and read out a Latin blessing upon "our liege lord, the Emperor, and upon the Senate, and upon the Order of Knights and upon the Commons of Rome and upon all sailors and all ships..." then he uttered the traditional Greek formula, "Ploiaphesia", meaning that vessels were now permitted to sail, to which the people responded with a loud cheer and dispersed happily to their homes, taking all kinds of decorations with them, such as olive boughs, scented shrubs and garlands of flowers, but first kissing the feet of a silver statue of the Goddess that stood on the temple steps.' (Apuleius, *The Golden Ass*, xi.)

The *Ploiaphesia* is well attested. In the region of Byzantium three centuries before this city became the capital of the eastern empire, the Ship of Isis was launched by its symbolic captain, a certain Artemidorus... We have the interesting names of 'captains' including two men named Socrates and women called Parthena, Isidora, Theapompis ('the lady of the sacred procession'), Isias (twice), Demetria and Paedeusis ('the lady professor')... The Ephiphany festival of the Eastern Church... involves a procession of priests and choir marching down to the water's edge. (Witt, *Isis in the Graeco-Roman World*, pp178, 184.)

The Zodiac of the main porch of the Cathedral of Notre Dame in Paris shows, linked to the sign of Aquarius, Isis launching a ship (the Isidis Navigium was known to have been celebrated in Paris). (Eisler, *The Royal Art of Astrology*, p269.)

12 March
[Helleno-Egyptian]
Hypatia, the Divine Pagan

Hypatia became the recognized head of the Neoplatonist School of Philosophy at Alexandria, and her eloquence, rare modesty and beauty, combined with her remarkable intellectual gifts, attracted a large number of pupils. The most notable, Synesius of Cyrene, made Bishop of Ptolemais in c.411, wrote affectionate and admiring letters to her asking advice on astronomy and mathematics, which are our main source of information on her.

She had been taught by her father, Theon, also a philosopher and geometer, who might well have been influenced by his contemporary, Pappus. (It was the famous theorem of Pappus which launched Pascal into Projective Geometry.) It is through this geometry that unevenly growing shapes, such as leaves and scallops, can best be drawn. According to legend, in March 415 AD Hypatia was scraped and sliced to death with cockle shells by the mad monks of the Nitre Desert of Libya — ostensibly because of her intimacy with Orestes, the city's Prefect. (It is thought the high nitrate content of their desert surroundings provoked an hysterical turn of mind, much as it later caused madness in hatters.) The cockle shell, associated with the birth of Aphrodite/Venus (because of the planetary number of striations in the shell — and its creation of the pearl), possibly for this celibate order of monks indicated the practice of ancient pagan philosophy and love rituals on the part of Hypatia. Yet she was one of those rare, harmonious persons able to understand the inner unity of the Classical and Christian teachings through philosophy and geometry, brilliantly sharing it, and inspiring

Figure 25   The terra cotta Venusian scallop shell in the British Museum.

love and devotion. She was held as an oracle for her wisdom, being consulted by magistrates in all important cases. Whatever the precise means, and motivation, for the murder, the departure soon afterward of many scholars from Alexandria marked the beginning of its decline as a major centre of ancient learning. (*Encyclopaedia Britannica*, 1810 and 1969 edns, and private research by Patricia Villiers Stuart.) [The Church today is no less adamant about refusing to make connections with their roots in the ancient world, and buries its head in the sand despite factual information of the type collected in this book, established by sound scholarship. Two Roman Catholic institutions approached for cult pictures of the Virgin Mary in daily use by congregations in Britain refused to allow them to be associated in this book with 'the Goddess of Pagan worship' — the very idea of which one priest described as 'offensive to our devotion'. We hope the Virgin's worshippers will on the contrary increase in number through using this book. We feel the Goddess herself, whatever Her name — would be far from offended: was the religion made for Her worship, or was it made for the convenience of Her priests? -Ed]

13 March
[Greek]

Diotima
A teacher of Socrates, described by him as 'a woman wise in this [love]

and in many other kinds of knowledge'. (Plato, *Symposium*, p201d.)

[Compare the importance of other women teachers who brought the Goddess dimension to the lives of the greatest philosophers: Aristoxenos tells us that Pythagoras received most of his moral views from the priestess of Delphi, Themistocleia.

Ibn al-Arabi in his *Futuhat al-Makkiyya* wrote that he was a disciple of a Gnostic, a lady of Seville called Fatimah bint ibn al-Muthanna of Cordova. 'I served her for several years, she being over ninety-five... She used to play on the tambourine and show great pleasure in it... She used to say to me, 'I am your spiritual mother and the light of your earthly mother;'. (Austen, *Sufis of Andalusia*, pp25~6.) -Ed]

15 March
[Anatolian]
Kybele/Rhea

Week-long purification for the Rites of Kybele on 22nd March begins, initiated by a procession of reed-bearers (*cannephori*). (Seyffert, *Dictionary*.)

Figure 26   Kybele on her lioness throne, shown here on a Roman coin from the Syrian 'City of Love', Hierapolis: courtesy of The Trustees of the British Museum.

19 March
Lesser Panathenaea/Quinquatria — Day One of Five Days
[Roman]
Athena

The Lesser Panathenaea was in later times moved to the spring, perhaps in consequence of Roman influence, in order to make it correspond to the Quinquatrus of Minerva. (Seyffert, *Dictionary*.)

In the lesser festivals there were three games conducted by ten presidents... On the evening of the first day there was a race with torches... The second combat was gymnastic, and exhibited a trial of strength and bodily dexterity. The last was a musical competition, first instituted by Perikles... There were besides the harp other musical instruments, on which they played in concert, such as flutes. The poets contended in four plays, the last of which was a satire. Whoever obtained the victory in any of these games was rewarded with a vessel of oil.. The conqueror also received a crown of olives which grew in the grove of Academus and were sacred to Minerva. (Lempriere, *Dictionary*.)

Figure 27   This small Greek bronze of the fifth century BC shows the self-born Athena in her characteristic martial stance — the Goddess as protectress of Athens: British Museum.

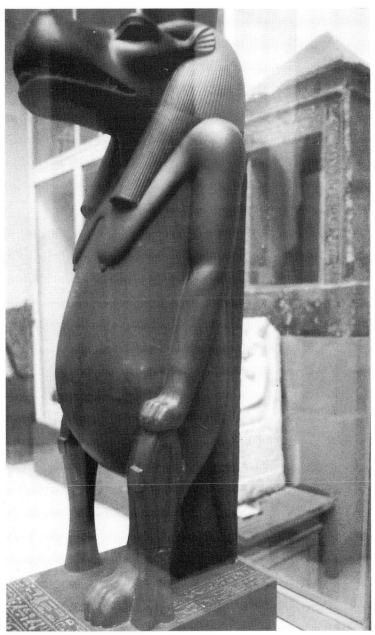

Figure 28 A seventh century BC schist statue of Isis as the Hippo Goddess of childbirth, Taweret, discovered buried at the Temple of Karnak, Thebes, appears on Egyptian zodiacs as the constellation Draco: Cairo Museum.

Minerva

The Quinquatrus, or the Birthday of Minerva, as its name implies, was celebrated in Rome five days after the Ides of March, though Ovid maintained it was so named because it lasted five days. (White, *Dictionary*.)

[The feast appears to have been a synthesis by the Romans of the five-*yearly* celebration of the Panathenaia into an annual one — see under 23 July — as well as a blending of the festival of Athena, celebrated by the Greeks in summer, with that of the Babylonian Ishtar in spring. The later Christian formulation of the spring equinox feast gives due place to each of the three Maries/Goddesses. -Ed]

'Rites are performed in honour of Minerva... Ye boys and tender girls, may you pray now to Pallas; he who shall have won the favour of Pallas will be learned. When once they have won the favour of Pallas, may the girls learn to card wool and unload the full distaffs. She also teaches how to traverse the upright warp with the shuttle, and she drives home the loose threads with the comb. Worship her, thou who dost remove stains from damaged garments; worship her, thou who dost make ready the brazen cauldrons for the fleeces. If Pallas frown, no man shall make shoes well, though he be more skilful than Tychius; and though he were more adroit with his hands than Epeus of old, yet shall he be helpless, if Pallas be angry with him. Ye too, who banish sicknesses by Phoebus' art, bring from your earnings a few gifts to the goddess. And spurn her not, ye schoolmasters... she attracts new pupils; and thou who dost ply the graving tool and paint pictures in encaustic colours, and thou who dost mould the stone with deft hands. She is the goddess of a thousand works: certainly she is the goddess of song; may she be friendly to my pursuits, if I deserve it.' (Ovid, *Fasti*.)

20 March

Lesser Panathenaea/Quinquatria — Day Two of Five Days

[Romano-Egyptian]

Isis

We may notice that in the Roman calendar the dates of the Quinquatria were from 19–23 March, but that on the second of the five days an Egyptian Festival was interposed called Pelusia, the theme of which was fundamental in the cult of Isis — securing the [next] annual inundation of the Nile by sympathetic magic. (Witt, *Isis in the Graeco-Roman World*, p123.)

ARIES

21 March
Spring Equinox
New Year's Day, Mesopotamia/
Persia/Palestine
— Day One of Eleven Days
Lesser Panathenaea/Quinquatria — Day
Three of Five Days

[Egyptian]
Seret, the Ewe
In 2791 BC on March 1st the sun entered the constellation Seret. The suffix 't' indicates the feminine gender, hence Aries was originally a ewe and not a ram. (Fagan, *Zodiacs Old and New*.)

[Greek]
Artemis
Artemis' favourite animal was held all over Greece to be the hind. From this sacred animal the month which the other Greeks called Artemi-

Figure 29 The cult statue of Diana of Ephesus flanked by hinds, as shown on a coin of the Roman Emperor, Hadrian: courtesy of The Trustees of the British Museum.

sion (March—April) was named by the Athenians Elaphe-bolion, and held her festival as goddess of game and hunting, at which cakes in the shape of deer were offered up. (Liddell & Scott, *Lexicon*.)

Tiamat

We know from the evidence of Babylonian ritual texts that both the spring and autumn equinoxes were the occasion of a New Year festival; at Uruk and Ur, for instance, this was so. But at Babylon the festival was held during the first eleven days of Nisan, in the spring, and the importance of Babylon led to the general observance of the festival in the spring [throughout the ancient Near East].

During the course of the festival *Enuma Anu Enlil* (the Epic of the Creation of the World) was recited twice, and it is probable that the series of rituals carried out were intended to be a dramatic re-enactment, with magical intent, of the main features of the Creation myth which the Epic embodies. These comprise a contest between Marduk and the Dragoness of Chaos, Tiamat... At some point in the myth... [Marduk] is slain and lies dead 'in the mountain', probably represented by the ziggurat, and is then restored to life by magical rites, in which the second chanting of the Epic has a part. (Hooke, *Babylonian and Assyrian Religion*, pp51-2.)

Figure 30   The Goddess of the Mountain, having emerged from her temple, is saluted in worship by a youth. She stands flanked by her lionesses holding out her staff of authority. Minoan ring sealing from Knossos, fifteenth century BC: Heraklion Museum, Crete.

22 March
New Year Festival, Mesopotamia/ Persia/Palestine
— Day Two of Eleven Days

Rites of Kybele — Day One of Six Days
Lesser Panathenaea/Quinquatria — Day
Four of Five Days
Maundy Thursday

[Mesopotamian]
Inanna/Ishtar/Belat

In the month of Nisan on the second day, after the *urigallu* priest has said this prayer, he shall open the door: the priests shall rise; they shall carry out their customary rituals before Bel and Belat. (Ritual text cited by Hooke, *Babylonian and Assyrian Religion*, p102.)

[Anatolian]
Kybele

After a week of fasting and purification the festival proper began. (*OCD*)

[Romano-Egyptian]
Isis/Bastet

We may well ask how much Christianity owes on the ceremonial side to the cult of Isis. To find the answer let us for a moment consider the case of Giordano Bruno in the late Renaissance. Bruno, who came to hold that the cross had been borrowed by Christians from the Egyptians, would be proud to know that the familiar black cassock and white surplice were worn in the service of Isis... The use of the rattle, certainly heard by him at church on a Maundy Thursday... could have made him think of the same instrument as used by women worshippers of Bast as well as Isis' own timbrel or sistrum... Bruno reborn might well contend that the very Inquisition... had done nothing to stop Pope Alexander VI from openly welcoming Isis as a cult figure in the Vatican. (Witt, *Isis in the Graeco-Roman World*, p276.)

[European]
Astarte/Aphrodite/Venus

The Gardens of Adonis (the dying or dead lover of Astarte/ Aphrodite/Venus) were baskets or pots filled with earth, in which wheat, barley, lettuces, fennel and various kinds of flowers were sown and tended for eight days, chiefly or exclusively by women... In Sicily Gardens of Adonis are still sown in spring as well as in summer... At the approach of Easter Sicilian women sow wheat, lentils and canary-seed in plates, which they keep in the dark and water every two days.

Figure 31   A bronze statuette of Bastet shows her with her worshippers as kittens, shaking Hathor's favourite musical instrument, the sistrum: British Museum.

The plants soon shoot up; the stalks are tied together with red ribbons, and the plates containing them are placed on the sepulchres... made up in Catholic and Greek churches on Good Friday, just as the gardens of Adonis were placed on the grave of the dead Adonis. The practice is not confined to Sicily... the whole custom may be nothing but a continuation under a different name of the worship of Adonis. (Frazer, *The Golden Bough*, pp341, 344.)

A correspondent of *The Times* in 1944 (April 13th) observed at Hammersmith on Maundy Thursday... little gardens on the pavement, each planted with twelve tiny shoots of privet and protected with branches.

Figure 32 A further Minoan ring sealing from Knossos symbolizes the death of Adonis by the uprooted tree, and his mourning by the women, one of whom collapses over an altar/tomb, holding harvested grain over her shoulder: Heraklion Museum, Crete.

These were, surely, 'Gardens of Adonis'... Once they were more elaborate, and rather like those to be seen in Sicily: a delicate sepulchre of shells and branches, with a candle burning inside. (Whistler, *English Festivals*, p113.)

23 March

New Year Festival, Mesopotamia/ Persia/Palestine
— Day Three of Eleven Days
Festival of Kybele — Day Two of Six Days
Lesser Panathenaea/Quinquatria — Day Five of Five Days
Good Friday

[Roman]

Minerva

'The last day of the five reminds us to purify the melodious trumpets and to make offering to the strong goddess.' (Ovid, *Fasti*, III, p849.)

[Palestinian]
Mary Magdalene

When the even was come, there came a rich man of Arimathaea, named Joseph, who also himself was Jesus' disciple.

He went to Pilate and begged the body of Jesus. The Pilate commanded the body to be delivered.

And when Joseph had taken the body, he wrapped it in a clean linen cloth

And laid it in his own new tomb, which he had hewn out in the rock: and he rolled a great stone to the door of the sepulchure and departed.

And there was Mary Magdalene, and the other Mary, sitting over against the sepulchre. (*Matthew* xxvii, 57.)

And Mary Magdalene and Mary the mother of Jesus beheld where he was laid. (*Mark* xv, 42.)

And the women also, which came with him from Galilee, followed after, and beheld the sepulchre, and how his body was laid.
And they returned, and prepared spices and ointments.

The hot cross buns of Good Friday, and the dyed eggs of Pasch or Easter Sunday, figured in the Chaldean rites just as they do now. The 'buns', known too by that identical name, were used in the worship of the Queen of Heaven, the Goddess Easter, as early as the days of Cecrops... 'One species of sacred bread', says Bryant (*Mythology* I, p373), 'which used to be offered to the gods, was of great antiquity, and called Boun.' Diogenes Laertius, speaking of this offering being made by Empedocles, describes the chief ingredients of which it was composed, saying, 'He offered one of the sacred cakes, called Boun, which was made of fine flour and honey.' The prophet Jeremiah takes notice of this kind of offering when he says, '...the women knead their dough, to make cakes to the Queen of Heaven' (*Jeremiah* vii, 18). The hot cross buns are not

Figure 33   Isis and Nephthys mourn over the bier of Osiris — as recorded by Mariette from a relief of the Ptolemaic period on the walls of the Osiris Chapel in the Temple of Hathor at Dendereh: courtesy The British Library.

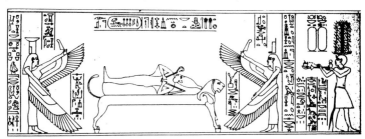

now *offered*, but *eaten*, on the festival of Astarte; but this leaves no doubt as to whence they have been derived. (Hislop, *The Two Babylons*, p107.)

Hecate/Artemis/Selene

In regard to hot cross buns on Good Friday, it may be stated that the Greeks offered to Apollo, Diana, Hecate, and the Moon, cakes with 'horns'. Such a cake was called a *bous* and (it is said) never grew mouldy. The 'cross' symbolized the four quarters of the moon. (Brewer, *Dictionary*.)

Even this most apparently Christian of minor customs cannot be claimed as a Christian invention... Wheaten cakes marked with a cross may have been eaten at the Spring Festival by all primitive peoples... They were certainly eaten wherever Diana was worshipped, and her festival occurred at this time. In Hertfordshire, where the Roman Ermine Street crosses the ancient Icknield Way, the ruins have been found of an altar raised to 'Diana of the Crossways'. Is it a coincidence that the neighbourhood has been noted for its Hot Cross Buns? (Ditchfield, *Old English Customs*.)

24 March

New Year Festival, Mesopotamia/ Persia/Palestine — Day Four of Eleven Days Festival of Kybele — Day Three of Six Days Easter Eve

[Mesopotamian]

Inanna/Ishtar/Belat

'In the month of Nisan on the fourth day, three and a half hours before the end of the night, the *urigallu* shall rise and wash himself with water from the river; he shall put on a linen garment... He shall go out from before Bel, then he shall recite this prayer to Belat: "She is mighty, she is divine; Zarpanit, the brightest of the stars, dwelling in the temple of Udul; the... of the goddesses, clothed with light; who dost pass through the heavens, dost keep up the earth; Zarpanit, whose dwelling is exalted; shining Belat, exalted and most high"' (Ritual text cited by Hooke, *Babylonian and Assyrian Religion*, p103.)

The ritual of the death and resurrection of Bel-Marduk is mentioned in the following fragmentary passage of Commentary, based on Zimmern's reconstruction and translation of the ritual commentary on Cuneiform tablet VAT 9555: 'That is Bel who is shut up in the Mountain... they seek for Bel, [saying] "Where is he held captive?" The [Goddess, his consort] stretches out her hands... The gate to which she comes is the gate of the grave. She enters and seeks him. The two who stand at the door of Esagila [the name of the ziggurat] are his guards — they are placed over him to guard him... he disappeared from life... the Goddess who remains with him, for his safety has come... that which is bound on the canopy of the Lady of Babylon is the head of the transgressor who went down with him; they slew him, his head is bound on the [canopy] of the Lady of Babylon... who went and returned to Borsippa, the canopy in which he is... the *mahhu* priest who goes before the Lady of Babylon, he is the messenger who weeps before her, "They have brought him into the mountain." She cries out thus, "My brother, my husband!" His garments which they bring to the Lady of Uruk (Inanna)... the milk which they... before Ishtar of Nineveh, because she nourished him, they show favour to her. *Enuma Anu Enlil* which they recite before Bel in Nisan, they sing it because he is imprisoned... The Lady of Babylon who [carried] black wool behind her and spotted wool in front of her...' (from Hooke, *idem*, p110.)

[Syrian]
Astarte/Venus Urania

For the rites of Venus Urania (Astarte) and Adonis at Byblos, all the people in mourning enter a deep cavern, where the image of a young man lies on a bed of flowers and odiferous herbs. Whole days are passed in prayers and lamentations. (Ramsay, *Les Voyages de Cyrus*, p205.)

Adonia were solemn feasts in honour of Venus, and in memory of her beloved Adonis. They lasted two days: on the first certain images of Venus and Adonis were carried, with all the pomp and ceremonies practised at funerals... Among the Egyptians, the Queen herself used to carry the image of Adonis in procession... The Egyptian Adonia are said to have been held in memory of the death of Osiris. (*Encyclopaedia Britannica*, 1810 edn.)

[Palestinian]

It may be conjectured that the motive of the Goddess in descending to the underworld was to bring back her youthful husband from the dead. This story of the Goddess Ishtar was [re-enacted] at the annual festival held in commemoration of the death of Tammuz, when women mourned for the dead god in Babylonia, as they mourned for him at

Jerusalem in the time of the prophet Ezekiel (vii, 14): 'then he brought me to the door of the house of Jehovah which was towards the north; and behold there sat women weeping for Tammuz'. (King, *Babylonian Religion and Myth*, p183.)

This account, more than any other, reveals that [Ezekiel] was observing the religion of Ashtoreth/Ishtar — still in practice at the temple in Jerusalem. (Stone, *Paradise Papers*.)

In the early Church the commemoration of the entombed Jesus appears to have fallen on exactly the same day as the requietio of Kybele and Attis, according to the Calendar of Silvius, written in 448.

Mary Magdalene

After two days was the Feast of the Passover, and of unleavened bread...

And being in Bethany in the house of Simon the leper, as [Jesus] sat at meat, there came a woman having an alabaster box of ointment of spikenard very precious; and she broke the box, and poured it on his head.

And there were some that had indignation within themselves, and said, why was this waste of ointment made?

For it might have been sold for more than three hundred pence, and have been given to the poor. And they murmured against her.

And Jesus said, Let her alone; why trouble ye her? She hath wrought a good work on me.

She hath done what she could: She is come aforehand to anoint my body to the burying. (*Mark* xiv, similarly *Matthew* xxvi.)

And behold, a woman in the city... when she knew that Jesus sat at meat in the Pharisee's house, brought an alabaster box of ointment,

And stood at his feet behind him weeping, and began to wash his feet with tears, and did wipe them with the hairs of her head, and kissed his feet and anointed them with the ointment. (*Luke*, vii, similarly *John* xii.)

There is in these accounts a noticeable similarity to the ritual of the mourning of Isis over the body of Osiris: on the death of Osiris 'the Goddess threw herself upon the coffin... they relate that she opened the chest and laid her face upon the face within and caressed it and wept'. (Plutarch, *De Iside et Osiride*, 357D.)

In the account in *John* Jesus is ministered to by the two sisters, Mary and Martha: in the same way Osiris is ritually attended and bewailed by the two sisters, Isis and Nephthys. Moreover, just as Jesus is anointed by Mary, so was the body of Osiris embalmed by Isis herself. (Plutarch, *De Iside et Osiride*.)

[Roman]

When we reflect how often the Church has skilfully contrived to graft the shoots of the new faith on the old stock of paganism, we may surmise that the Easter celebration of the dead and risen Jesus was grafted upon a similar celebration of the dead and risen Adonis, which... was celebrated in Syria at the same season. The type created by Greek artists of the sorrowful goddess with her dying lover in her arms, resembles, and may have been the model of, the *Pieta* of Christian art...

In this connection a well-known statement of Jerome may not be without significance. He tells us that Bethelehem... was shaded by a grove of that still older Lord, Adonis, and that where the infant Jesus had wept, the lover of Venus was bewailed. Though he does not expressly say so, Jerome seems to have thought that the grove of Adonis had been planted by the heathen after [Jesus'] birth. (Frazer, *The Golden Bough* abdgd, p345.)

It was after the rebellion of Bar Cochba that the Roman Emperor established the Mysteries of Adonis at the Sacred Cave in Bethlehem... The rites of Venus and Adonis appear also to have been celebrated in Jerusalem itself, after that city had been rebuilt by the Romans as Aelia Capitolina. (Blavatsky, *Isis Unveiled*.)

'The priestesses of Venus are often seen to weep at the annual festival of Adonis.' (*Ammianus Marcellus*, XIX i, 11.)

[European]
The Corn Mother

The rituals of the Corn Mother and the Corn Daughter in Northern Europe are best seen in the district of Bruck in Styria, Austria. The last sheaf of corn, called the Corn Mother, is made up into the shape of a woman by the oldest married woman in the village, of an age from fifty to five-five years. The finest ears are plucked out of it and made into a wreath which, twined with flowers, is carried on the head of the prettiest girl in the village... On Easter Eve the grain is rubbed out of

Figure 34 A seal design from Khafaje, Mesopotamia, shows a priestess and king (or goddess and priest/priest and priestess), taking the sacred drink through straws before enacting the sacred marriage, symbolized by the scorpion.

it by a seven-year-old girl and scattered amongst the young corn... Here the fertilizing power of the Corn Mother is plainly brought out by scattering the seed taken from Her body among the new corn; and her influence over animal life is indicated by placing the straw in a manger. (Frazer, *Golden Bough* abgd, p400.)

25 March
New Year Festival, Mesopotamia/ Persia/Palestine — Day Five of Eleven Days Anglo-Saxon New Year Festival of Kybele — Day Four of Six Days Easter Day

Inanna/Ishtar/Belat

'In the month of Nisan, on the fifth day, four hours before the end of the night, the *urigallu* shall rise, and shall wash himself with water from the river, with water from the Tigris and the Euphrates — he shall go in before Bel and Belat and invoke them by the names of the stars... Two hours after sunrise, when the table of Bel and Belat have been set in order, the *urigallu* shall summon a *mashmashu* (exorcist) who shall purify the temple... the exorcist shall remain in the midst of the court. He shall not enter into the chapel of Bel and Belat.' (Ritual text cited by Hooke, *Babylonian and Assyrian Religion*.)

During the annual New Year's festival, when the king took upon himself the humiliations and splendours of the God Marduk, there was enacted the liberation of the deity from his mountain prison within the Ziggurat, after a search through the city by his mourning Goddess, in which all the people joined. Later the resurrected God in the king's person mounted the stairways to the chapel on the summit... within which was [to be] consummated the sacred marriage. (Levy, *The Phoenix' Nest*, p116.)

Astarte

What means the term Easter itself?... It is nothing other than Astarte, one of the titles of Belat, the Queen of Heaven, whose name as pronounced by the people of Nineveh, was evidently identical with that now in common use in this country. That name, as found by Layard on Assyrian monuments, is Ishtar. The worship of Bel and Astarte was very early introduced into Britain, along with the Druids... If Bel was thus worshipped in Britain, it will not be difficult to believe that his consort Astarte was also adored by our ancestors, and that from Astarte whose name in Nineveh was Ishtar, the religious solemnities [of the spring], as now practised, are called by the name of Easter — that month, among our Pagan ancestors, having been called Easter-month...

The popular observances that still attend the period of its celebration amply confirm the testimony of history as to its Babylonian character. The hot cross buns of Good Friday, and the dyed eggs of Pasch or Easter Sunday, figured in the Chaldean rites just as they do now... the egg became the symbol of Astarte of Easter; and accordingly, in Cyprus, in one of the seats of the worship of Venus, or Astarte, an egg of wondrous size was represented... Besides the mystic egg, there was also another emblem of Easter, the Goddess Queen of Babylon, and that was the Rimmon, or Pomegranate. In this country, and most of the countries of Europe, no pomegranates grow; and yet, even here, the superstition of the Rimmon must as far as possible be kept up. Instead of the pomegranate, therefore, the orange is employed and so the [Roman Catholics] of Scotland join oranges with their eggs at Easter. (Hislop, *The Two Babylons*, pp103, 110.)

[Persian]

Easter Eggs, or Pasch Eggs, are symbolical of creation, or the recreation of Spring. The practice of presenting eggs to our friends at Easter is Magian or Persian, and bears allusion to the World Egg... There is

Figure 35   A procession of maidens bearing egg, flower and pomegranate before the seated Demeter. Relief from the Harpy Monument, Lycia, Turkey, fifth century BC: British Museum.

Figure 36 Kybele with a young lion on her lap holds the cone and bowl, symbols of the sacred marriage. Fourth century BC, found at Piraeus: Berlin Museum.

a tradition also that the world was 'hatched' or created at Easter-tide. (Brewer, *Dictionary*.)

[Syrian]

Venus Urania

Suddenly the grief changes to joy; happy chants replace the laments; everywhere this hymn is intoned: 'Adonis has come back to life; Urania weeps no more; he is ascended to heaven!' (Ramsay, *Les Voyages de Cyrus*, p206.)

It was formerly a common belief that the sun danced on Easter Day. (Brewer, *Dictionary*.)

[Roman]
Kybele

On the 25th of March, which was reckoned the vernal equinox, the divine resurrection was celebrated with a wild outburst of glee. It was the festival of Joy (Hilaria). (Frazer, *Golden Bough*, p350.)

Amid tumultuous music, and rites of wildest sorrow, they sought and mourned for Attis on the mountains. On the third day he was found again, the image of the Goddess was purified from the contagion of death, and a feast of joy was celebrated as wild as had been the days of sorrow. (Seyffert, *Dictionary*.)

(See illus. 36: Kybele with the symbols of the sacred marriage.)

'O Mother of gods and men... O life-giving Goddess that art the counsel and the providence and the creator of our souls... O thou that givest all good things... do thou grant to all men happiness, and that chief happiness of all, the Knowledge of the Gods!' (Julian, *Hymn to the Mother of the Gods*, 166C.)

[Palestinian]
Mary Magdalene

It is noticeable in the Death and Resurrection rites of the great pre-Christian religions that the god is always accompanied by a goddess. Osiris is attended by Isis, Tammuz by Ishtar, Bel-Marduk by Belat-Ishtar, Adonis by Venus, Attis by Kybele. In each case the goddess is shown, either explicitly or implicitly, as restoring the god to life.

In the accounts of the death, burial and ressurrection of Jesus the person most in evidence is Mary Magdalene, or an unnamed woman traditionally identified with her.

On the search by Mary Magdalene for the body of Jesus, 'only some inhibition or mistaken reverence can prevent us from being reminded of Aphrodite, seeking and weeping for Adonis' (White, *God and the Subconscious*, p219). Similarly, Ishtar of Babylon is reflected in Mary Magdalene. Among the epithets of the great Babylonian goddess are 'Goddess of Love', and 'The Great Harlot'. So Mary Magdalene, like her Babylonian prototype, is traditionally represented as a courtesan. Another correspondence may be noticed in the inscription of the Akkadian King Sargon: 'As a gardener, the Goddess Ishtar loved me', as compared with the description of Mary Magdalene, 'She turned herself back, and saw Jesus standing... She, supposing him to be the gardener..' (*John* xx, 14.)

Significant parallels are also to be seen between Isis and Mary. One of the emblems of Isis is the *auxilaria*, or ritual pot — the name refers to the Goddess's providence in helping her devotees (Apuleius, *The*

Figure 37 Mary Magdalene holding the sacred vessel of unguent which symbolizes the ineffable mystery of her shaktic womb. Fifteenth century fresco by Piero della Francesca, Arezzo Cathedral, Italy.

Golden Ass). Similarly, one of the most characteristic attributes of Mary Magdalene is the alabaster box, mentioned in *Matthew, Mark* and *Luke*. The magical use to which Isis puts her hair is mentioned in the *Book of the Dead*. 'Thou spreadest out thy hair and I shake it out over his brow' is spoken concerning Isis who 'hideth in her hair and draweth her hair over her'. In the accounts both in *Luke* and *John* Mary wipes the feet of Jesus with her hair.

Isis in her reanimation of Osiris, embalms his body, bringing the murdered god to eternal life: so also Mary anointed Jesus 'beforehand for his burial' and after his death helped to prepare spices and ointments. Proserpine is said to have restored Adonis to life on condition that he spend six months with her and the rest of the year with Venus.

[Romano-Egyptian]
Isis/Kybele

The spring festivals of Isis and Kybele took place in Egypt generally in March, just as Lady Day, or the first great festival of Kybele, was held in the same month in pagan Rome... the common title of Kybele at Rome was 'Domina', or 'Lady', as in Babylon it was Belat ('Lady'), and from this, no doubt, comes the name Lady Day as it has descended to us. (Hislop, *The Two Babylons*, p103.)

[Palestinian]
The Lady Mary

Lady Day: The pagans claimed that the Church had copied their most sacred rites by placing her Holy Week at the vernal equinox. Frazer has recently defended the position saying that the commemoration of Jesus' death was placed by a great many churches upon March 25th to replace the celebration of Attis' death on the same date. (Cumont, *Oriental Religion*, pp70, 228.)

[English]

At the Roman Hilaria, and in the North under other names, honour had been done to the Mother of the Gods. But names did not mean very much in that England. The baptized pagan, still a pagan at heart, was content to bring his gifts to another building, or to the same building furnished with different symbols... He honoured the idea of motherhood, and his descendants in Protestant England, especially in the western counties, continued to honour that idea in their mothers' house. On that Sunday, the fourth in Lent, they would visit her with a trinket or a bunch of early flowers. (Whistler, *English Festivals*, p105.)

[English]

Eostre/Easter

Baeda derives the word from *Eostre* (Northumberland spelling of Eastre), a goddess whose festival was celebrated at the vernal equinox. (*OED*)

Waes hael ('be whole, be well'): Wassail was a salutation used on New Year's Eve and New Year's Day over the spiced-ale cup, hence called the 'wassail bowl'. The civil and legal year began on March 25th until after the alteration of the style, in 1752, when it was fixed, like the historic year to January 1st. In Scotland the legal year was changed to January 1st as far back as 1600. (Brewer, *Dictionary*.)

26 March

New Year Festival, Mesopotamia/ Persia/Palestine — Day Six of Eleven Days Festival of Kybele — Day Five of Six Days Easter Monday

Kybele

In the Calendar of Philocalus, written in 354, the day following the Hilaria is a day of rest, the Requietio.

Demeter and Persephone

You may bring back the life of spring in the form of a tree or a maiden, or you may summon her to rise from the sleeping Earth. In Greek mythology we are most familiar with the Rising-up form. Persephone, the daughter of Demeter, is carried below the earth, and rises up again year after year. On Greek vase paintings the scene occurs again and again. A mound of earth is represented, sometimes surmounted by a tree; out of the mound a woman's figure rises. (Harrison, *Art and Ritual*, p78.)

[Irish]

The Grey Woman of Crotlieve

Father J.B.Mooney tells me that the Grey Woman on Crotlieve used to be elaborately dressed up like a woman for the Easter festivities. The Grey Woman of Crotlieve appears to be a pillar stone set up in prehistoric times. (Danaher, *The Year in Ireland*.)

27 March

New Year Festival, Mesopotamia/ Persia/Palestine — Day Seven of Eleven Days
Festival of Kybele — Day Six of Six Days

Kybele

The festival closed on the twenty-seventh of March with a procession to the brook Almo. The image of the Goddess, with its face of jagged black stone, sat is a wagon drawn by oxen. Preceded by the nobles walking barefoot, it moved slowly, to the loud music of pipes and tambourines, out by the Porta Capena, and so down to the banks of the Almo, which flows into the Tiber just below the walls of Rome. There the high priest, robed in purple, washed the wagon, the image, and the other sacred objects in the waters of the stream. On returning from their bath (the *Lavatio*), the wain and the oxen were strewn with fresh spring flowers. All was mirth and gaiety. (Frazer, *Golden Bough* abgd, p351.)

(On the arrival of the Emperor Julian at Callinicum in Mesopotamia in the year 363): 'There, on the twenty-seventh day of March, the day on which at Rome the annual procession in honour of the Mother of the Gods takes place, and the carriage in which her image is carried is washed, as it is said, in the waters of the Almo, he celebrated the usual rites in the ancient fashion.' (*Ammianus Marcellus*, XXIII, pp3, 7.)

28 March

New Year Festival, Mesopotamia/ Persia/Palestine — Day Eight of Eleven Days

Ishtar

(A prayer for the healing of a sick man): 'In the month of Tammuz, when Ishtar causes the people of the lands to weep for Tammuz, her husband, then, when the families of humankind are gathered together there, Ishtar appears, and, beholding the situation of humankind, takes away sickness and causes sickness. ... On the twenty-eighth day of the month, the day of sheep-folds, thou shalt offer a vulva of lapis-lazuli, and a golden star to Ishtar; thou shalt name the name of the sick man, and say, "Deliver the sick man..."' (quoted in Hooke, *Babylonian and Assyrian Region*, p33.)

29 March

New Year Festival, Mesopotamia/ Persia/Palestine — Day Nine of Eleven Days

Inanna/Ishtar/Belat

The most significant rite of the New Year was the *hieros gamos*, or holy marriage between the king, who represented the god Dumuzi, and one of the priestesses, who represented the Goddess Inanna... the idea arose that the king of Sumer, no matter who he was or from what city he originated, must become the husband of the life-giving goddess of love, that is, Inanna of Uruk... the role of the priestess of Inanna was that of the dominant partner, since She makes him king [and] She is asked as the Queen of Heaven to allow him to enjoy long days at Her holy lap. (Stone, *Paradise Papers*, p152.)

The very important ceremony of the Sacred Marriage... probably took place in a chapel on the summit of the ziggurat. (Hooke, *Babylonian and Assyrian Religion*, p52.)

[Greek]

Basilissa

The most important ceremony of the Anthesteria, a moveable feast held

Figure 38   A Syrian cylinder seal, when rolled out on clay, shows a local king paying homage to Venus (Inanna/Ishtar) who in return bestows upon him his regal authority. c. Fifteenth century BC: Pierpoint Morgan Library, New York.

February/March, was the marriage of the Basilissa or wife of the Archon Basileus, with Dionysos, the Basilissa being regarded as representing the country. The ceremony took place in the older of the two temples of the Lenaeon, which was never opened except on this occasion. (Seyffert, *Dictionary*, p190.)

[Roman]

Nerine

From the work of Joannes Lydus on the Roman calendar we know that on 23 March there was a festival of Mars and Nerine, the Sabine goddess whom people identified with Athena (Minerva) or Aphrodite (Venus)... We may conclude that it represents a marriage of Mars to Nereine. (Frazer, on Ovid's *Fasti*, p409.)

30 March

New Year Festival, Mesopotamia/ Persia/Palestine — Day Ten of Eleven Days

Inanna/Ishtar/Belat

Then there was a procession along the Sacred Way from Esagila to the *bit-akitu*, or Festival House outside the city; in this the king took the hand of Marduk, to lead the god out at the head of the procession, followed by all the visiting gods, the priests and the populace. (Hooke, *Babylonian and Assyrian Religion*, p52.)

31 March

New Year Festival, Mesopotamia/ Persia/Palestine — Day Eleven of Eleven Days Jewish Ecclesiastical New Year

Mammitu/Tiamat

The remaining features of the ritual were a ceremony called 'the fixing of destiny', determining the prosperity of the New Year.
(Hooke, *Babylonian and Assyrian Religion*, p52.)

Mammitu was the Goddess of Fate, responsible for the fixing of destinies.

(Pinches, *Religion of Babylon and Assyria*, p94, and Sandars, *Epic of Gilgamesh*, Glossary.)

[The Fixing of Destinies probably involved the casting of the horoscope of the king and therefore of Mesopotamia as a whole, at the point the old year ended and the new year began at the end of the eleventh day: it would thus be easy to read from the chart what the destiny of the kingdom would be for the coming year, and what had been ordained by the positions of the planets against the stars at that moment. As we see at the beginning of the festival, Time/Tiamat first had to be brought under control by Marduk. On the last day of that festival, that control bore fruit, in that to some extent the future could be predicted and prepared for, ensuring the smooth running of the kingdom. -Ed]

'The Mamit! The Mamit! The Treasure which passeth not away!... a shape of salvation descending from the midst of the heavenly abyss.' (Massey, *Tracts*.)

There are various accounts given... in the early Babylonian tradition, Tiamat swallows the god Marduk and it is perhaps in reference to this that we read that Marduk 'looked upon the womb of Tiamat... and Kingu who had taken his place therein'. In the Creation Narrative there is mention of a 'return to her womb', but it seems uncertain as to what or whom this applies. A later tradition stated that Marduk temporarily maintained his independent position, but even then his battle is renewed year after year. He meets afresh every year and every day on the confines of earth and heaven the scorpion-men of Tiamat, the fish with heads of men, and goats and many more... Tiamat is never conquered... Almost the last verses of the Hymn of Praise exhort Tiamat (but they do not command her) to 'recede into the future... until time of old'. (Durdin-Robertson, *Goddesses of Chaldaea*, p4.)

[Thracian]
Bendis

Bendis was a goddess of the moon amongst the Thracians. She was invested with power over heaven and earth, and identified by the Greeks with Artemis, Hecate and Persephone. The worship of this Goddess was introduced into Attica by Thracian aliens; and was so popular that in Plato's time it became a state ceremonial at Athens. A public festival was instituted called the Bendideia, at which there were torch-races and a solemn procession of Athenians and Thracians at the Piraeus. (Seyffert, *Dictionary*.)

[Roman]
Luna

The Italian Goddess of the Moon had in Rome an ancient sanctuary

Figure 39 A second century painted alabaster carving of the Moon Goddess from Hatra, Mesopotamia: courtesy the Iraqi Cultural Centre, London.

on the Aventine, in which as Goddess of the month she received worship on the last day of March, which was the first month of the old Roman year. (Seyffert, *Dictionary*.)

1 April
[Roman]
Venus/Concordia/Fortuna

The goddess Concordia was invoked with Venus and Fortuna by married women at the Veneralia on the 1st of April. (Seyffert, *Dictionary*.)

'Duly do ye worship the Goddess, ye Latin mothers and brides, and ye, too, who wear not the fillets and long robe [courtesans]. Take off the golden necklaces from the marble neck of the Goddess; take off her gauds; the Goddess must be washed from top to toe. Then dry her neck and restore to it her golden necklaces; now give her other flowers, now give her the fresh-blown rose. Ye, too, she herself bids bathe under the green myrtle... Learn now why ye give incense to Fortuna Virilis in the place which reeks of warm water. All women strip when they enter that place... Propitiate her with supplications; beauty and fortune and good fame are in her keeping.' (Ovid, *Fasti*, IV, p133.)

A barbarous custom from pagan times is still established in Ireland, namely, to make an April Fool of a person. At the time when Venus was worshipped the first day of the month was a festival in her honour, and it was customary to play all sorts of low pranks to do her veneration. (Danaher, *The Year in Ireland*, p84.)

4 April
The Megalesia — Day One of Seven Days
[Anatolian/Roman]
Kybele

The Megalesia was a festival in honour of the Magna Mater, celebrated annually on the 4th of April with processions and games. (Cicero, *Fam.* 2.11.2.)

The Megalesia (Festival of the Great Mother) is so called from the Greek *Megale Meter*, because by direction of the Sibylline Books the Great Mother was brought from King Attalus from Pergama; there near the city wall was the Megalesion, that is, the temple of this goddess, whence she was brought to Rome. (Varro, *Ling.Lat* VI, 15.)

'Straightway the Berecynthian flute will blow a blast on its bent horn, and the festival of the Idaean Mother will have come... the Goddess herself will be borne with howls through the streets in the city's midst. The stage is clattering, the games are calling... I am daunted by the shrill cymbal's clash and the bent flute's thrilling drone. "Grant me, Goddess, someone whom I may question"... I was about to ask why the Megalesia are the first games in the year in our city, when the Goddess (i.e. the Muse Erato) took my meaning and said, "She gave birth to the Gods. They gave place to the Parent, and the Mother has the honour of precedence"' (Ovid, *Fasti*, IV, 179.)

5 April

The Megalesia — Day Two of Seven Days

Kybele

According to the [Sibylline] oracle the holy stone image of Kybele was received at Ostia by the first citizen of the land, an honour accorded

Figure 40   Kybele/Rhea riding on her lioness, a painted Greek terracotta.

to Scipio Nasica — and carried by the most esteemed matrons to the Palatine, where, hailed by the cheers of the multitude and surrounded by fumes of incense, it was solemnly installed... A temple was erected to her on the summit of the Palatine, and every year a celebration enhanced by scenic plays, the *Ludi Megalenses*, commemorated the date of dedication of the sanctuary and the arrival of the Goddess. (Cumont, *Oriental Religion*, p47.)

7 April

The Megalesia — Day Four of Seven Days

Claudia Quintia, Priestess of Kybele

The Muse Erato tells of the coming of Kybele's image: 'She had arrived at Ostia, where the river Tiber divides to join the sea and flows with ampler sweep. All the knights and the grave senators, mixed with the common folk, came to meet her at the mouth of the Tuscan river. With them walked mothers and daughters and brides, and the virgins who tended the holy hearths. The men wearied their arms by tugging lustily at the rope... Yet the ship stuck fast, like an island firmly fixed in the middle of the sea. Astonished at the portent, the men did stand and quake. Claudia Quinta, whose beauty matched her nobility... stepped forth from the procession of chaste matrons and... thrice lifted her palms to heaven (all who looked on her thought she was out of her mind), and bending the knee she fixed her eyes on the image of the Goddess, and with dishevelled hair uttered these words: "Thou fruitful Mother of the Gods, graciously accept thy suppliant's prayers..." She spoke, and drew the rope with a slight effort... The Goddess was moved, and followed her leader... Attended by a crowd, Claudia walked in front with joyful face... The Goddess herself, seated in a wagon, drove in through the Capene Gate; fresh flowers were scattered on the yoked oxen. Nasica received her.' (Ovid, *Fasti*, IV, 291.)

8 April

The Megalesia — Day Five of Seven Days

Claudia Quintia, Priestess of Kybele

'Claudia took off her girdle and fastened it about the prow of the ship, and like one divinely inspired, bade all stand aside; and then she besought the Goddess... And lo, she not only made the ship move, but even towed her for some distance up stream. Two things, I think the Goddess showed the Romans on that day; first that the freight they were bringing from Phrygia was... truly divine, not lifeless clay, but a thing of life and divine powers... And the other was that no-one of the citizens could be good or bad and she not know thereof.' (Julian, *Hymn to the Mother of the Gods*, 159D.)

9 April

The Megalesia — Day Six of Seven Days

Kybele

[In the ancient world, a conical black stone represented The Great Goddess at her temples in leading cult centres like Alexandria, Byblos, Emesos and Paphos. Clement of Alexandria states that it was characteristic of the Arabs to worship cult stones. The Arab writer, Dhu al-Khalasa states that a square stone represented Allaat, the Arab version of Kybele. The most celebrated of these Goddess stones still in use today is the black stone retained from Arabia's pre-Islamic era, framed in silver and set into the side of the Ka'aba (a cubic temple) at Mecca. The word 'Ka'aba' in Arabic also means 'Virgin', and refers to the Goddess as the Unmanifest Substance from which all forms are born. Amongst the many rituals retained from the ancient world required of worshippers who make the pilgrimage to Mecca, the custom is retained of kissing the stone and praying for any dearest wish to be granted. -Ed]

Figure 41   The climactic act of the many rituals required of worshippers at the Ka'aba, Mecca, is to kiss the Black Stone, the most ancient element in the structure. This night view shows them circling in thousands round it, in the way pre-Islamic Arabians would have done.

10 April

The Megalesia — Day Seven of Seven Days
[Roman]

Kybele

When the next Dawn shall have looked on victorious Rome, and the stars shall have been put to flight and given place to the sun, the Circus will be thronged with a procession and an array of the deities, and the horses, fleet as the wind, will contend for the first palm. (Ovid, *Fasti*, IV, 389.)

12 April

The Cerealia — Day One of Eight Days
[Roman]

Ceres

The Cerealia were games introduced at the founding of the temple of Ceres. Those held in later times were given by the aediles from 12-19 April, and another festival to Ceres, held in August, was established. Just as the Patricians entertained each other with mutual hospitalities at the Megalesian games, so did the Plebeians at the Cerealia. (Seyffert, *Dictionary*.)

13 April

The Cerealia — Day Two of Eight Days
[Roman]

Ceres

'Next come the games of Ceres. There is no need to declare the reason; the bounty and services of the Goddess are manifest. The bread of the first mortals consisted of the green herbs which the earth yielded without solicitation; and now they plucked the living grass from the turf, and now the tender leaves of tree-tops furnished a feast. Afterwards the acorn was produced... Ceres was the first who invited man to better sustenance and exchanged acorns for more useful food. She forced bulls to yield their necks to the yoke; then for the first time the upturned soil beheld the sun... Ceres delights in peace; and you, ye husbandmen, pray for perpetual peace and for a pacific prince. You may give the Goddess spelt, and the compliment of spurting salt, and grains of incense on old hearths; and if there is no incense, kindle resinous torches. Good Ceres is content with little, if that little be but pure... White is Ceres'

Figure 42   Kore, Grain Goddess of Life and Death, is symbolized on these classical coins by a female-headed tomb out of which sprout both the wheat-ear of life and the poppy of death (from G. Radet: Cybebe, courtesy The British Library).

proper colour: put on white robes at Ceres' festival.' (Ovid, *Fasti*, IV, 393.)

15 April

The Thesmophoria — Day One of Five Days
The Cerealia — Day Four of Eight Days
[Greek]

Demeter

Thesmophoria, a surname of Ceres as law-giver, in whose honour festivals were instituted called Thesmophoria... Three days were required for the preparation. (Lempriere, *Dictionary*.)

The Thesmophoria, a festival to Demeter, as the foundress of agriculture and of the civic rite of marriage, celebrated in many parts of Greece, but especially at Athens. It was held at Athens from 9 to 13 Pyanepsion... Two of the wealthiest and most distinguished women were chosen out of every district to preside over the festivals; their duty was to perform the holy functions in the name of the others, and to prepare the festal meal for the women of their own district. (Seyffert, *Dictionary*.)

The Thesmophoria took three days, and the first one was called Kathodos or Anodos: this was when the women went down into caves. (Shuttle and Redgrove, *The Wise Wound*, p182.)

'With regard to the mysteries of Demeter, which the Greeks call the Thesmophoria, I know them, but I shall not mention them, except so far as may be done without impiety. The Danaids brought these rites from Egypt, and taught them to the Pelasgic women of the Peloponnese... in Arcadia, where the natives remained and were not compelled to migrate, their observance continued.' (*Herodotus*, II, p171.)

[Roman]

Tellus Mater

The Italian deity of mother-earth was held on 15th April to ensure plenty during the year, and was celebrated under the management of the *pontifices* and the Vestal Virgins, partly on the Capitol in the thirty *curiae*, and partly outside the town. (Seyffert, *Dictionary*.)

The Earth Goddess. Conservation. Respect for the environment. (*Fellowship of Isis Directory*.)

Figure 43   One of many Earth mother figures, understood literally as an obese seated or lying female, found in fourth to third millennia period temples in Malta: Valletta Museum, Malta.

16 April

The Thesmophoria — Day Two of Five Days (Preparatory)
The Cerealia — Day Five of Eight Days [Greek]

Demeter

The Thesmophoria were nothing else but the periods of the Greek women elevated to an annual festival, as Kerenyi remarks... among the Greeks we know that it was thought that women independently of men were able during these days to promote the earth's fertility. The rites were developed for this purpose... It is probable that the origin of this festival was indeed a specifically menstrual mystery. The women, who according to some authorities, invented agriculture, did so because only they had the secret of the strong fertility of the seed corn. The reason for this was that originally the women mixed the seed corn with menstrual blood, which was the best possible fertilizer, before planting it. Since the men had no magic blood of this kind, they could not grow corn as well as the women could, any more than they could grow babies. (Shuttle and Redgrove, *The Wise Wound*, p184.)

[Palestinian]
Bath-Kol/Filia Vocis

The nubile maiden in the her first menstruating phase is referred to as *rtu* (law) in Sanskrit... In the Hebrew tradition the Bath-Kol (Daughter of the Voice) is a cognate symbol. The Voice originated as the Vak (voice) of female puberty and gestation. (Grant, *The Magical Revival*, p123.)

17 April

The Thesmophoria — Day Three of Five Days
The Cerealia — Day Six of Eight Days
[Greek]

Demeter

After the assembly had met in the temple of Ceres, the women shut out all the men and dogs, themselves and the bitches remaining in the temple all night: in the morning, the men were let in. (Alexander, *History of Women*, I, p73.)

The Attic Thesmophoria appears to have represented with mourning rites the descent of Persephone into the lower world, and with joy her return... Hence the Descent or Ascent variously applied to the first, and the name Kalligeneia (fair-born) to the third day of the festival.

Upon the 11th of the month called Pyanepsion, the women went to Eleusis, carrying books on their heads, in which the laws which the Goddess had invested were contained. (Lempriere, *Dictionary*.)

18 April

The Thesmophoria — Day Four of Five Days
The Cerealia — Day Seven of Eight Days
[Greek]

Demeter

The second day of the Festival proper was a fast. (*OCD*)

[When Demeter visited the house of Celeus and Metaneira] some women were in the house, and when they bade her sit down beside them, a certain old woman, Iambe, joked with the Goddess and made her smile. For that reason they say that the women tell dirty jokes at the Thesmophoria. (Apollodorus, *Bibliotheca*, I,v.)

In the Syracusan Thesmophoria, the participants carried *mylloi*, cakes made of honey and sesame in the shape of the female sex organ. (Neumann, *The Great Mother*, p265.)

19 April

The Thesmophoria — Day Five of Five Days
The Cerealia — Day Eight of Eight Days

Demeter

The name *Kalligeneia* (fair-born) was applied to the third day of the Thesmophoria. (Frazer, *Golden Bough* abgd, p469.)

It was usual during the festival to offer prayers to Ceres, Proserpine, Pluto and Kalligeneia... all persons whose offence was small were released from confinement. (Lempriere, *Dictionary*.)

'Pray ye now to Demeter and the Divine Maiden, the Holy Twain; pray ye to Pluto, and to the mother of all beauty, the fruitful nourishing Earth! Pray ye to Hermes and the Graces.' (Aristophanes, *Thesmophoriazusae*, I,2.)

TAURUS

21 April
[Greek]

Io

Some poets have called the stars of Taurus Io. They also varied the title by the equivalent Juvenca Inachia (the Inachian Heifer or Maiden). The word may refer to the Egyptian 'Iw', 'Cow'. (Eisler, *Royal Art of Astrology*, p93.)

[Roman]

Vacca, the Cow

But whether this sign is a cow or a bull it is not easy to know; the forepart is visible, the hinder part is hid. (Ovid, *Fasti*.)

Aphrodite/Venus

Taurus was considered under the guardianship of Venus... whence it was known as *Veneris Sidus*, *Domus Veneris nocturna*, and *Gaudium Veneris*: an idea also, perhaps, influenced by its containing the Pleiades, the Doves, the favourite birds of that goddess. (Allen, *Star Names*, 383.)

Pales

The Palilia was a festival celebrated by the Romans in honour of the Goddess Pales... This festival was observed on the 21st of April, and it was during the celebration that Romulus first built his city. (Ovid, *Fasti*.)

'Night has gone and Dawn rises. I am called upon to sing of the Palilia and not in vain shall be the call if kindly Pales favours me. O kindly Pales, favour me when I sing of pastoral rites... Sure it is I have leapt over the flames ranged three in a row, and the moist laurel bough has sprinkled water on me... Ye people, go fetch materials for fumigation from the Virgins' altar. Vesta will give them; by Vesta's gift ye shall

Figure 44   Aphrodite, ruler of Taurus, holds her symbols of dove and pod (or bud). The limestone relief dates from the sixth century BC, and comes from a sanctuary on the island of Thasos: Louvre, Réunion des Musées Nationaux.

be pure... Shepherd, do thou purify the well-fed sheep at fall of twilight; first sprinkle the ground with water. Deck the sheepfold with leaves and branches fastened to it. Adorn the door and cover it with a long festoon. Make blue smoke with pure sulphur, and let the sheep, touched with the smoking sulphur, bleat. Burn... olives and pine and savines, and let the singed laurel crackle in the midst of the hearth. And let a basket of millet accompany cakes of millet; the rural goddess particularly delights in that food. Add viands, and a pail of milk, such as she loves; and when the viands have been cut up, pray to Sylvan Pales, offering warm milk to her. Say... "Ward off from my stalls all harm. O let it flee away! If I have fed my sheep in holy ground, or sat me down under a hallowed tree... if the nymphs and the half-goat god have been put to flight at sight of me; if my pruning-knife has robbed a holy copse of a shady bough ... pardon my fault... forgive it, nymphs, if the trampling of hoofs has made your waters turbid. Do thou, goddess, appease for us the springs and their divinities; appease the deities dispersed through every grove... Drive far away all diseases: may men and beasts be hale, and hale too the sagacious pack of watch-dogs. May I drive home my flocks as numerous as they were at morn... Avert dire hunger. Let grass and leaves abound, and water both to wash and drink. Full udders may I milk; may my cheese bring me in money; may the sieve of wicker-work give massage to the liquid whey. And let the wool grow so soft that it could not fret the skin of girls nor chafe the tenderest hands. May my prayer be granted, and we will year by year make great cakes for Pales, the shepherds' mistress!" With such things is the goddess to be propitiated; these things pronounce four times, facing the east, and wash thy hands in living dew. Then mayest thou get thee a wooden bowl to serve as mixer, and mayest quaff the snow-white milk, and purple must; anon leap with nimble foot and straining thews across the burning heaps of crackling straw.' (Ovid, *Fasti*.)

Dea Roma

'Our good friend Lucius Tarutius of Firmum, who was steeped in Chaldaic lore, made a calculation based on the assumption that our city's birthday was on the Palilia... and from that calculation even went so far as to assert that Rome was born when the moon was in the sign of Libra and from that fact unhesitatingly prophesied her destiny.' (Cicero, *De Div.* II, xlvii.)

'As for the day they began to build the city, it is universally agreed to have been the twenty-first of April, and that day the Romans annually keep holy, calling it their country's birthday... Yet before ever the city was built, there was a feast of herdsmen and shepherds kept on this day, which went by the name of Palilia [or Parilia].' (Plutarch, *Lives*, Romulus.)

After the second century of our Era the festival was combined with that of *Dea Roma*, and was celebrated as her birthday with festal processions and Circensian games, which continued until the 5th century... Between the old Forum and the Colosseum Hadrian erected a handsome double temple in honour of Roma and Venus, as ancestress of the Roman people. This was consecrated on April 21st. (Seyffert, *Dictionary*.)

23 April
[Roman]
Venus of the Vinalia

There were two Vinalia festivals, on April 23 when the wine of the previous year was broached and a libation from it poured on the sod; and on August 19th. With both festivals was associated the worship of Venus, who, as goddess of gardens, had vineyards also under her protection. (Seyffert, *Dictionary*.)

'I have told of Pales, I will now tell of the festival of the Vinalia; but there is one day interposed between the two. Ye wenches of the people, celebrate the divinity of Venus: Venus favours the earnings of ladies of a liberal profession. Offer incense and pray for beauty and popular favour; pray to be charming and witty; give to the Queen her own myrtle and the mint she loves, and bands of rushes hid in clustered roses. Now is the time to throng her temple next the Colline gate; the temple takes its name from the Sicilian hill... Venus was transferred [from Eryx in Sicily] to Rome in obedience to an oracle of the long-lived Sibyl, and chose to be worshipped in the city of her own offspring.' (Ovid, *Fasti*, iv, p863.)

[European]

In Eastern Europe many analogous rites to the Parilia have been performed down to recent times, and probably still are performed for the same purpose, by shepherds and herdsmen on St George's Day, the 23rd of April, only two days after the Parilia, with which they may well be connected by descent from a common festival observed by pastoral Aryan peoples in the spring... On St George's Day, which is the modern equivalent of the Parilia, Southern Slavonian peasants crown their cows with wreaths of flowers... in the evening the wreaths are... fastened to the door of the cattle-stall, where they remain throughout the year until the next St George's Day. With the offerings and the prayer that accompanied them at the Parilia [see Ovid's prayer for 21st April], we may compare the ritual which herdsmen in the Highlands of Scotland used to observe and the prayers which they used to utter at Beltane, the festival which is the Celtic analogue of the Italian Parilia... In Pennant's account of the Beltane festival the spilling of the caudle (composed partly of milk) on the ground answers to the offering of milk to Pales, and the Highland herdsman's prayer to the being who preserved his flocks and herds corresponds to the prayer which the Italian shepherd addressed to Pales, as we learn from the following verses of Ovid. Tibullus tells us that it was his wont to purify his sheep herd every year and to sprinkle Pales herself with milk, referring no doubt to the libation of milk to the goddess at the Parilia.

Perhaps Ovid's expression, 'when the viands have been cut up' is explained by the Beltane custom, described by Pennant, of breaking a cake of oatmeal in pieces and throwing the bits over the shoulder as offerings to the preservers or destroyers of the flocks and herds. Among the viands so cut up at the Parilia were no doubt included the millet cakes mentioned by Ovid in a previous line... Such a displacement of two days in the adjustment of Christian to heathen celebrations occurs in the festivals of St George, Assumption of the Virgin, and at Easter. (Frazer, *Golden Bough* abgd, pp415, 360.)

28 April

Floralia — Day One of Six Days [Roman]

Flora

Originally a Sabine goddess of the spring and of flowers and blossoms in general, to whom prayers were offered for the prospering of the ripe fruits of the field and tree. She was also regarded as a goddess of the flower of youth and its pleasures. [Probably descended from the Greek Chloris], her worship was said to have been introduced into Rome by the Sabine King Titus Tatius, and her special priest, the *Flamen Floralia*, to have been appointed by Numa... A theatrical festival, the *Floralia*, was instituted in 238 BC at the behest of the Sibylline books. At this feast the men decked themselves and their animals with flowers, especially roses; the women put aside their usual costume and wore gay dresses. The scene was one of unrestrained merriment. From 173 BC the festival was a standing one and lasted six days from 28th April, the anniversary of the foundation of the temple, to 3 May. For the first five days of the games, for the superintendence of which the *curule aediles* were responsible, there were theatrical performances, largely consisting of very lewd farces called mimes. The people were regaled during the games with porridge, pease and lentils. (Seyffert, *Dictionary*.)

29 April

Floralia — Day Two of Six Days

Flora

'When the spouse of Tithonus (i.e. Aurora)... thrice has lifted up her radiant light in the vast firmament, there comes a goddess decked with garlands of a thousand varied flowers, and the stage enjoys a customary licence of mirth.' (Ovid, *Fasti*, IV, p943.)

'Cicero was a serious-minded man and by way of being a philosopher. When he was entering on the aedileship he shouted out, in the hearing of the whole citizen body, that among the other duties of his office it fell to him to propitiate Mother Flora by the holding of games.' (Augustine, *De Civitate Dei*, II, p27.)

30 April

Floralia — Day Three of Six Days
Beltane Eve/May Eve

[European]

May Day Eve is the day for children to gather spring flowers and hang May baskets. This is the Eve of Beltane, the ancient Celtic May Day festival, when great bonfires were kindled and the cattle were blessed. (*Druids Calendar*.)

[Spanish]

The last day of April was also a time set apart for the cult of the dead. At a short distance to the eastward of the entrance into the passage of the dolmen of Equilaz, the ground shows signs of having been subjected to the action of fires. This fact is accounted for, says Signor Antonio Pirala, by the bonfires which used to be lit at the tombs in honour of the dead, on the last day of April. (Borlase, *Dolmens*, II, p694.)

[German]

St Walpurga

On Walpurgis Night was the eve of May Day, when the old pagan witch-world was supposed to hold high revelry... on certain high places. The Brocken of Germany was a favourite spot for these revelries. (Brewer, *Dictionary*.)

The title and character of the Witches' Sabbath on the summit of the Brocken, on the night between April 30th and May 1st, spring equally from the old and the new religion. Walpurga was the sister of Saints Willibald and Wunnibald, and emigrated with them from England to Germany in the eighth century. As Abbess of a Convent at Heidenheim in Franconia [she] became one of the most popular saints, not only in Germany, but also in Holland and England. (Bayard-Taylor, on Goethe's *Faust*, p226.)

St Walpurga was a Sussex-born woman saint who emigrated to Germany. Interestingly, Walburg is an old Teutonic name for the Earth

Mother. (Farrar, *What Witches Do*, p96.)

In the 18C German map-makers usually... gave a short description of the Brocken, the highest peak of the Hartz Mountains, stating that at the summit was the famous 'Witches' Ground' where the Sabbats take place, and close to it an altar, which was formerly consecrated to a pagan god. There was also a spring of water here, and both the spring and altar were used in the witches' ceremonies... it is evidently an old sacred

Figure 45 A winged Lilith in clay from the Old Babylonian period c. 1800 BC, known as the Burney Relief, stands with bird feet on lions, flanked by owls. She holds in either hand the line and circle of measurement: on loan from Mr Goro Sakamoto to the British Museum.

mountain, on the summit of which pre-Christian rites took place. (Valiente, *ABC of Witchcraft*, p47.)

Lilith

According to Babylonian mythology Lilith is an embodiment of men's night sexual dreams, appearing as the dominant, devouring partner. Hence in Jewish thought Lilith was associated with undesirable female power as linked with sexuality, and is often depicted as the Serpent in the Garden of Eden. Understood as Adam's second wife, she is the female principle as the Shakti, with more energy and power than her husband. Eve on the other hand embodies the female principle subservient to Adam. [Ed.]

To Helena Blavatsky, Lilith in physiological terms manifests as the *aura clitoridis*. The image of Inanna/Isis sitting with wide-open legs, sometimes on a pig, continues into Greek and Latin where the female genitals are called 'pig'... Baubo, whose obscene dance cheered the mourning Goddess and made her laugh, appears even in the supreme mystery of Eleusis. (Shuttle and Redgrove, *The Wise Wound*, p205.)

The charm to avert the Evil Eye is called in Italian 'the fig', synonym for the female genitals. The gesture made is *mano in fica*, made by closing all the fingers into a fist, and thrusting the thumb between the first and second fingers, representing the clitoris in the labia. (Valiente, *ABC of Witchcraft*, p112.)

Figure 46   Inanna with parted legs: a fourth millennium seal from Ur, Mesopotamia, prototype of the Irish Sheela na-Gig.

1 May

Floralia — Day Four of Six Days
May Day
[Carthaginian/Phoenician]

Tanit

Tanit is the Phoenician moon goddess, whose worship, it was claimed,

Figure 47 A second century Punic limestone votive relief to Tanit, surrounded by planetary symbols: British Museum.

was still carried out in Cornwall and the West of England, being celebrated by ritual bonfires on the old pagan festival dates. (Valiente, *ABC of Witchcraft*, p66.)

It is possible that the great Celtic festival of Beltane, on May 1st, may derive its name from the first two deities of the Carthaginian Triad, *Baal*-Hammon, *Tanit* and Eshmun. The Irish word for fire, *teine*, closely resembles the Carthaginian *tine*, which is regarded as a gift of Tanit (Venus Urania). (Durdin-Robertson, *Goddesses of Chaldea*, p133.)

The first day of May was the beginning of Summer. It was pronounced *Bel-ti-na*, the name for the 1st of May still always used by speakers of Irish. (Dineen, *Dictionary*.)

The Convocation of Visneach... was kept upon the first day of May... Upon this occasion they were used to kindle two fires in every territory of the kingdom... It was a solemn ceremony at this time to drive a number of cattle of every kind, between these fires, this was conceived to be an antidote and a preservation against the murrain, or any other pestilential distemper among cattle, for the year following. (Keating, *General History of Ireland*.)

Danu/Danann

The Tuatha Dea Danann came to Ireland on Monday, the kalends of May, in ships. (*Lebor Gabala Erenn*, IV, p141.)

The *Tuatha Dea Danann* signifies 'the people of the Goddess Danu or Danann', who was the Mother of the Gods... According to our bardic chronicles the Dedannans were the fourth of the prehistoric colonies that arrived in Ireland many centuries before the Christian era. They were magicians, and highly skilled in science and metal-working. After inhabiting Ireland for about two hundred years, they were conquered by the people of the fifth and last colony — the Milesians (i.e. Gaels). When they had been finally defeated... they held secret council, and arranged that the several chiefs, with their followers, were to take up residence in the pleasant hills all over the country — the *side* or elf-mounds — where they could live free from observation or molestation. (Joyce, *Social History of Ireland*, I, p251.)

Beltane was another day anciently dedicated to fetes in honour of the dead and fairies. (Evans-Wenz, *Fairy-Faith*, p439.)

Drink from a well before sunrise. Wash in the morning dew, and adorn yourselves with greenery... watch the sun come up, dance round the Maypole, and otherwise abandon yourself to the season. A woodland frolic culminating in indiscretion is the order of the day. (*Druids Calendar*.)

According to ancient belief... nothing makes beautiful like kissing the dew on May morning. People have held that belief in the present century. As for Mrs Pepys in an earlier one, she thought it 'the only thing in the world to wash her face with', and got up every year at four o'clock to do it. Some used even to run a silver spoon through the grass, and bottle it... Mention must be made of the Milkmaid's garland... a glittering trophy of silver utensils, fixed to a cloth-covered pyramid, carried about like a sedan chair on poles. (Whistler, *English Festivals*, p143.)

The ancient people, with their deeper insight into the spiritual processes in nature, recognized this dew as a magical substance bearing the essence of the Earth. (McLean, *Four Fire Festivals*, p19.)

[Assyrian]
Luna

The moon tree is often shown in pictures... In one Assyrian relief it has ribbons like our Maypole. Perhaps a dance may have taken place around the tree in those faraway days, like the dance that is still performed round the Maypole on May Day. In such a dance the ribbons would be interwoven, as in our own dance, to represent the decking of the bare tree with bright-coloured leaves and flowers and fruits, all gifts of the moon goddess, giver of fertility. (Harding, *Women's Mysteries*.)

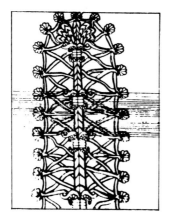

Figure 48   The Assyrian Sacred Tree may be a symbol of the days of the lunar month. Certainly the lunar year was central to their calendar: numerous renditions appear on the eighth century BC reliefs of the Palace of Ashurnasirpal at Nimrud, now in the British Museum.

[Palestinian]
Asherah

The central role of the Maypole and Christmas tree in vegetation rites has been well known... We know of the veneration in which the tree cult was held among the Semites — the tree cult of the heights; the worship of the cult pole of Asherah, the goddess of heaven; and the ritual dance around the tree. (Neumann, *The Great Mother*, p259.)

The sacred pole as the symbol of Ishtar, or Astarte, or any other form of the mother goddess, is everywhere to be found in the ancient Near East. (Hooke, *Babylonian and Assyrian Religion*, p33.)

[English]

Guinevere

Malory relates that when Queen Guinevere advised her knights of the Round Table that on the morrow (May Day, when fairies have special power) she would go a-maying, she warned them all to be well-horsed and dressed in green. This was the colour that nearly all the fairy-folk of Britain and Ireland wear. It symbolizes, as many ancient mystical writings declare, eternal youth and resurrection and rebirth, as in all nature during the springtime. (Evans-Wenz, *Fairy Faith*, p312.)

The May Queen

'A choir of bright beauties in spring did appear,
To choose a May-lady to govern the Year.'

(Dryden, Lady's Song.)

In the south-east of Ireland on May Day the prettiest girl used to be chosen Queen of the district for twelve months. She was crowned with wild flowers; feasting, dancing, and rustic sports followed, and were closed by a grand procession in the evening. During her year of office she presided over rural gatherings of young people at dances and merry-making. (Frazer, *Golden Bough* abgd, p131.)

In Kent and Sussex, traditionally there is a May Queen chosen from the pupils at one of the junior schools, who is crowned and decked in a long white cloak and carries a garland of flowers. Usually she has a number of attendants, even a May King in some places, although it is really her day. She... is a representation of the White Goddess, the Earth Mother in her Maiden aspect. In ancient times there was a sacred festival... The ordinary folk would spend the night before the feast in the woods, gathering green branches and flowers to deck a bower for the Queen and King... Sometimes after this dance everyone would go out into the fields with garlanded sticks and broom handles covered with flowers and leap high, singing and dancing, to make the corn grow tall. (Green, *A Harvest of Festivals*, p138.)

The early English consecrated May-day to Robin Hood and Maid Marian... Stow says that the villagers used to set up May-poles and spend the day in archery, Morris-dancing and other amusements. (Brewer, *Dictionary*.)

In Sussex the May Pole... used to be topped with a large birch broom. A 'besom' is a dialect term used for a [loose] female... and the female genitals were known vulgarly as 'the broom'. To 'have a brush' was to have sexual intercourse. This throws considerable light on the real significance of the broomstick in witch rituals, and in old folk-dances, in which it often plays a part. (Valiente, *ABC of Witchcraft*, p48.)

In the 1930s there would still be villages where the Maypole would be danced around. (Whistler, *English Festivals*, p142.)

[Roman]

Bona Dea

The Good Goddess was an Italian goddess supposed to preside over the earth, and all the blessings which spring from it... The anniversary of the foundation of her temple was held on the first of May, when prayers were offered to her for the averting of earthquakes. (Seyffert, *Dictionary*.)

Maia, Maia Maiestas

Maia was one of the Pleiades... The Romans identified her with an old Italian goddess of Spring. She was held to be the wife of Vulcan, to whom the *flamen* of that god made offering on the 1st of May. (Seyffert, *Dictionary*.)

Dea Dia

Was probably a goddess of the cornfields. A college of priests consisting of twelve life-members performed her worship... their badge was a white fillet and a wreath of ears of corn. Named the *Arvales*, they held their chief festival on three days in May, on the 1st and 3rd in Rome, and on the 2nd in the grove with a highly complicated ceremonial, including a dance in the temple of the goddess, to which they sang the written text of a hymn so antiquated that its meaning could scarcely be understood. (Seyffert, *Dictionary*.)

The *Fratres Arvales* college consisted of twelve members chosen from the most distinguished senatorial families by co-optation; the reigning Emperor was always a member... The most important ceremony of this brotherhood took place in May in honour of the goddess Dea Dia to whom the grove was dedicated. The rites of this agricultural cult belong to an early stage of Roman religion. (*OCD*)

Flora

Polydore Virgil says that the Roman youths used to go into the fields and spend the kalends of May in dancing and singing in honour of Flora, goddess of fruits and flowers. (Brewer, *Dictionary*.)

The May baskets of flowers and the Maypole came from the Roman *Floralia*, the festival of flowers. The Romans welcomed the month of May by dedicating the month to Flora, the Roman flower goddess... Roman children made little images of Flora and decorated them with flowers on this day. As Christian celebrations began to replace the pagan festivals, these May dolls were turned into likenesses of the Virgin Mary. (*Unicorn Gardens*, Beltane 1980.)

[Romano-British]

Flora

Sometimes two circles, intersecting and bound with blossom, were fixed to the top of a staff, wound spirally with flowers in the manner of the classical thyrsus. In Rutland... garlands of this kind were made by children very early in the morning, from flowers they had picked the evening before. The same device may have been used at the Floralia in Roman Britain, the festival of Flora, goddess of flowers, heralded in Rome with a braying of trumpets. For Roman remains have been found in the neighbourhood of King's Lynn, and here, in the last century, these formal emblems were carried about the town with a great deal of monotonous hooting on cows' horns. The two hoops were crossed on the point of a staff, and bound with bunches of flowers interspersed with evergreens... [on top of which] were bright-coloured flying ribbons. Below, on the centre of the globe, was a doll fixed to the top of the staff, her name being long since forgotten. It may have been Flora herself. It was certainly the local goddess of flowers. (Whistler, *English Festivals*, p144.)

[European]

Flora

The later orgiastic use of the hawthorn... corresponds with the cult of the Goddess Flora, and... accounts for the English mediaeval habit of riding out on May Morning to pluck flowering hawthorn boughs and dance around the maypole. Hawthorn blossom has, for many men, a strong scent of female sexuality; which is why the Turks use a flowering branch as an erotic symbol. Mr. Cornish proves that this Flora cult was introduced into the British Isles in the first century by the second Belgic invaders. (Graves, *The White Goddess*, p176.)

In Russian Lithuania, on the first of May, they used to set up a green tree before the village. Then the rustic swains chose the prettiest girl, crowned her, swathed her in birch branches and set her beside the May-tree, where they danced, sang, and shouted, 'O May! O May!' (Frazer, *Golden Bough*, abgd, p126.)

3 May

Floralia — Day Six of Six Days

Flora

'"Come, Mother of Flowers, that we may honour thee with merry games; last month I put off giving thee thy due. Thou dost begin in

Figure 49   Rembrandt's mistress, Saskia, painted as the Goddess Flora in the seven-teenth century: courtesy The Trustees of the National Gallery, London.

April and passest into the time of May..." So I spoke, and the goddess
answered my questions thus, and while she spoke, her lips breathed
vernal roses: "I who now am called Flora was formerly Chloris: a Greek
letter of my name is corrupted in the Latin speech. Chloris I was, a
nymph of the happy fields where, as you have heard, dwelt fortunate
men of old. Modesty shrinks from describing my figure... I enjoy
perpetual spring; most buxom is the Year ever; ever the tree is clothed
with leaves, the ground with pasture. In the fields that are my dower,
I have a fruitful garden, fanned by the breeze and watered by a spring
of running water. This garden my husband filled with noble flowers
and said, 'Goddess, be Queen of Flowers'. Oft did I wish to count the
colours in the beds... Soon as the dewy rime is shaken from the leaves,
and the varied foliage is warmed by the sunbeams, the Hours assemble, clad in dappled garments, and cull my gifts in light baskets.
Straightway the Graces draw near, and twine garlands and wreaths to
bind their heavenly hair. I was the first to scatter new seeds among
the countless peoples... Perhaps you may think that I am queen only
of dainty garlands; but my divinity has to do also with the tilled fields.
If the crops have blossomed well, the threshing-floor will be piled high;
if the vines have blossomed well, there will be wine; if the olive-trees
have blossomed well, most bounteous will be the Year... Honey is my
gift. It is I who called the winged insects, which yield honey, to the
violet, and the clover, and the grey thyme... We delight in festivals and
altars... if we are neglected, we avenge the wrong... I myself was once
neglected by the Roman Senate. What was I to do? By what could I
show my resentment? What punishment exact for the slight put on me?
In my gloom I relinquished my office. I guarded not the countryside,
and the fruitful garden was naught to me. The lilies had dropped; you
might see the violets withering, and the tendrils of the crimson saffron
languishing... I did not will it so, nor am I cruel in my anger; but I
did not care to ward off these ills. The Senate asembled and voted an
annual festival to my divinity if the Year should prove fruitful. I accepted the vow. The consuls Laenas and Pstumius celebrated the games
which had been vowed to me."

'But why is it that whereas white robes are given out at the festival
of Ceres, Flora is neatly clad in attire of many colours? Is it because
the harvest whitens when the ears are ripe, but flowers are of every
hue and every shape? She nodded assent, and at the motion of her
tresses the flowers dropped down, as falls the rose cast by a hand upon
a table... She vanished into thin air. A fragrance lingered; you could
know a goddess had been there.' (Ovid, *Fasti*, V, 183.)

Bona Dea

A secret festival was held for her on behalf of the public welfare, in
the house of the officiating consul or praetor of the city, by matrons
and the Vestal Virgins, on the night of May 3-4. The mistress of the

house presided... the women performed a dance, accompanied by wind and stringed instruments. (Seyffert, *Dictionary*.)

The festivals were celebrated only in the night by the Roman matrons... all the statues of the men were carefully covered with a veil where the ceremonies were observed. (Lempriere, *Dictionary*.)

The room was decorated with vine-branches and other plants and flowers... Wine was brought in, but called milk, and the covered jar containing it a honey-pot. (*OCD*)

It being evening... [Cicero] went to the house of a friend and near neighbour; for his own was taken over by the women, who were celebrating with secret rites the feast of the goddess whom the Romans call the Good, and the Greeks the Women's Goddess. For an offering is annually performed to her in the consul's house, either by his wife or mother, in the presence of the Vestal Virgins. (Plutarch, *Lives* (Cicero))

Cornelius Labeo regarded [Bona Dea] as an Earth Goddess, identical with Maia, Fauna, Ops, and Fatua; he affirmed that her character as an Earth-goddess was proved by the secret rites observed in her honour, and that she was involved in the books of the pontiffs under the titles Good, Fauna, Ops and Fatua. Her identification with the old Roman Goddess Maia, who gave her name to the month of May, may have arisen from the accident that both were worshipped on May Day. According to Festus, the Good Goddess was also called Damia, her priestess bore the title Damiatrix... This points to an identification or confusion of the Good Goddess with the Greek goddess Damia, a divinity of growth and fertility akin to Demeter. (Frazer, *Commentary*.)

'But far off we heard the laughter of cloistered maids, where a holy grove made a dark encircling wood, the secret place of the Goddess of Women, with holy fountains and rites... Wreaths of purple veiled its portals far withdrawn, and a hut shone with sweet fire of incense. A poplar decked the shrine with far-spread leaves, and its deep foliage shielded singing birds.' (*Propertius* IV ix, 23.)

4 May
[Irish]

St Monica

In his well-documented study, *Historic Thorn Trees in the British Isles*, Vaughan Cornish writes of the sacred hawthorns growing over wells in Goidelic provinces. [At such a one] in Tin'ahely in County Wicklow, devotees attended on 4th May, rounds were duly made around the well, and shreds torn off their garments and hung on the thorn. Plainly, since

St Monica's Day, New Style, corresponds with May 15th Old Style, this was a ceremony in honour of the Hawthorn month, which had just begun. (Graves, *The White Goddess*, p175.)

8 May
[Cornish]
Flora

Helston in Cornwall has from time immemorial been noted for a popular festival held annually on 8th May, called 'the Furrey', supposed to have been derived from the Roman Floralia, or games in honour of the goddess Flora: on this occasion persons parade the streets with garlands of flowers, and all ranks partake of the pleasures of dancing and various rural amusements. (Lewis, *Topographical Dictionary of England*.)

The name 'Furrey' is possibly derived from the Latin word *feria*, meaning a fair or holy day, usually of a religious nature... Another popular name is Flora Day, or the Floral Dance, under which name the written words of the song are usually known. This would relate to Flora, the Roman goddess of the spring and flowers, and was popularly used in Helston... Of the song sung at the festival five verses are sung today: the first deals with Robin Hood and Little John. Traditional heroes of Britain, Robin Hood and his Merrie Men appear in many guises in folk plays, and Maid Marian is another version of the Goddess of the Woodlands and Wildthings. (Green, *A Harvest of Festivals*, pp23-8)

Julian of Norwich
Born May 8th c. 1417.

13 May
[Portuguese]
Our Lady of Fatima

At the first of Her Appearances after an unexpected flash of lightning, on 13 May 1917, three shepherd children of Fatima saw Mary in a gleaming white robe, wearing a crown of roses, floating above an oak tree.

14 May
[Graeco-Egyptian]
Isis

The Panegyric of Isis to be addressed in Pachons (May):

Remembering your gifts, men to whom you have granted
wealth and great blessing

All duly set aside for you one tenth of these blessings,
rejoicing each year at the time of the Panegyric.

Thereafter you allow everyone, as the year rolls round,
to rejoice in the month of Pachons.

Joyful after your festival, they return home reverently filled with the sense of blessedness that comes only from you.

If you are present here too, you witness individual virtue, delighting in the oblations, libations and offerings of
the men who dwell in the Province of Suchos, the Ar-
sinoites, men of mixed races who all, yearly, are present at
Pachons and Thoth, bringing a tenth for you, and Sokonop-
sis most sacred of gods, at Your feast.

O Hearer of prayers, black-robed Isis, the Merciful, and
ye Great Gods who share the temple with her, send Paeon
to me, healer of all ills.

(Isidoros, Hymns II, 21 and III, 28.)

*Figure 50   Carved in schist in the twenty-sixth dynasty, the Goddess Isis, crowned
with cobras, protects with her wings her husband Osiris, manifesting as the immortal
being of any spiritually evolved human: British Museum.*

15 May
[Roman]

Vesta

Where the sacred fire of the moon is tended by Vestal priestesses, they are usually responsible also for the rain rituals... Just as in ancient Rome the Vestal Virgins, guardians of the sacred fire of Vesta, performed a ceremony at the Idea of May, the time of the full moon, to regulate the water supply. (Harding, *Women's Mysteries*, p128.)

GEMINI

21 May

[Egyptian]

Tefnut

In the Dendereh Zodiacs the Twins are represented by the air-god Shu, and his wife and sister Tefnut, the feline goddess of moisture. (Budge, *Gods of the Egyptians* II, p312.)

[Mesopotamian]

Eve

Christians said that the stars of Gemini together represented Adam and Eve, who probably were intended by the nude male and female figures walking hand in hand in the original illustration in the Alphonsine Tables. (Allen, *Star Names*, 224.)

[Greek]

Leda

While on earth the Twins were the sons of Leda. (Allen, *Star Names*.)

[Roman]

Maia Maestas

The Romans identified Maia with an old Italian goddess of spring who was held to be the wife of Vulcan. (Seyffert, *Dictionary*.)

The Muses answer Ovid's question as to the origin of the name of the month of May: 'Majesty (Maiestas) who regulates the whole world... was great on the very day she was born. Without delay she took her seat high in the midst of Olympus, a golden figure far seen in purple vestment.' (Ovid, *Fasti* V, 9 and 25.)

Figure 51   Tefnut, Goddess of Moisture, was portrayed as a feline by the Egyptians, since without moisture there is no life, and the lioness symbolized Life: British Museum.

Maeve

Maeve is the most truly Venusian of the strong Celtic goddesses. It is for her that hawthorn was named May, or May-thorn. She became the goddess of Beltane in whose honour the May queen was crowned... Her most recent name in English lore is Queen Mab of the fairies. (Denning and Phillips, *The Magical Philosophy* III, p163.)

[Palestinian]
The Virgin Mary

Though Catholics at large were not imitating the Carmelites in detail, they treated the whole of May as, in a general sense, Mary's month. (Ashe, *The Virgin*, p201.)

24 May
[French]
The Three Maries

At Arles, in Provence, the cult of the Goddess as a Triad or Pentad of Mothers has survived under Christian disguise until today, when her festival is celebrated from May 24 to May 28. Now her devotees are largely gypsies. As a Triad she has become known as 'The Three Maries of Provence', or 'The Three Maries of the Sea'; as a Pentad she has had Martha added to her company, and an apocryphal serving-girl called Sara. (Graves, *White Goddess*, p191.)

In the Sepher Yetzirah, one of the oldest of the Kabalistic Books whose authorship is attributed to Abraham, we find the idea of a Feminine Trinity in the first place, from whom a Masculine Trinity proceeds; or, as it is written in the text: 'Three Mothers whence proceed Three Fathers'. (Blavatsky, *The Secret Doctrine* V, p211.)

The female triad was brought on as the three Maries of the Christian mythology. The triad of this name was found on a tablet at Metz with the inscription, *In honorem domus divinae Dis Mairabus, vicani vici pacis* (In honour of the divine house, to the Goddesses Mariae, they of the Street of Peace). Montfaucon held them to be divinities of the country, and therefore extant before the Christian era. (Massey, *The Natural Genesis* I, p535.)

Victoria

Born on May 24 1819, Queen Victoria was in her lifetime worshipped as their chief divinity by a sect in Orissa. (Frazer, *Golden Bough* abgd, p100.)

The Lama Kazi Dawo-Sandup told me that, because Tibetans saw the likeness of Queen Victoria on English coins and recognised it as being that of Dolma, there developed throughout Tibet during the Victorian Era a belief that Dolma had come back to birth again to rule the world in the person of the Great Queen of England; and that, owing to this belief, the British Representatives of the Queen then met with an unusually friendly reception in their negotiations with Lhassa, although probably unaware of its reason. (Evans-Wentz, *Tibetan Book of the Dead*, p116.)

Figure 52 The three-fold goddess was sculpted at Hatra in the second century with Anat/Athena as the central figure: Iraq Museum.

31 May

Century Games — Day One of Three Days
The Feast of Our Lady, Queen of Heaven [Roman]

Proserpine

There were saecular games held by the Romans only once in a century... in honour of Pluto and Proserpine, and were instituted in obedience to the Sibylline verses, which promised that 'the empire should remain in safety so long as this admonition was observed'. (Brewer, *Dictionary*.)

The Saecular Games were performed by the Roman State to commemorate the end of one *saeculum* and the beginning of a new. The saeculum, defined as the longest span of human life, was fixed in the republic as an era of a hundred years [other sources say one hundred and ten]. The celebration... ceremony took place in the Campus Martius, near the Tiber, at a spot which was known as Tarentum. The gods honoured... were Dis (Pluto) and Proserpine, who had an altar nearby.

Figure 53   A Hellenistic relief showing Pluto and Persephone, King and Queen of the Underworld: courtesy of The Trustees of the British Museum.

Augustus' Games of 17 BC are well known from Horace's *Carmen Saeculare*, and from an inscription, found near the Tiber, which gives details of the complicated ritual. They consisted of three nights and three successive days of archaic scenic games, and of seven supplementary days of more modern entertainment in theatre and circus. Each night Augustus and Agrippa made appropriate offerings... beside the Tiber... (*OCD*)

The Games here described conform to the ritual created in 17 BC by Augustus and followed by all his successors; it is very different from the primitive ritual, which was concerned essentially with the chthonian divinities Dis and Proserpine; Augustus includes other divinities in the festival, and adds numerous elements of Greek origin... The Games start on the night of the 31st May/1st June; it is then that takes place the offering to the Moerae celebrated by the Emperor... also, on the same night... one hundred and ten matrons celebrate the *Sellisternia*, a holy meal offered to the goddesses Juno and Diana, whose statues are placed on seats; during the same night also are given sacred representations in a theatre. (Paschoud, Commentary to Zosimus, *Historia Nova*.)

When the time of the festival which is celebrated in the Field of Mars for three days and as many nights, has come, offerings are dedicated on the bank of the Tiber, at Tarentum; they are made to the following deities: to Zeus, to Hera, to Apollo, to Leto, to Artemis, and especially to the Moerae, to the Eileithyiae, to Demeter, to Hades and to Persephone. (Zosimus, *Historia Nova*, II v, 2.)

'O Phoebus, O Diana, Queen of forests, radiant glory of the heavens, O ye ever cherished and ever to be cherished, grant the blessings that we pray for at this holy season when the verses of the Sibyl have commanded chosen maidens and spotless youths to sing the hymn in honour of the deities who love the Seven Hills...
'O goddess, bless the ancestral edicts concerning wedlock... destined, we pray, to be prolific in new offspring, that the sure cycle of ten time eleven years may bring round again music and games thronged thrice by bright daylight and as often by gladsome night!
'And ye, O Fates (Parcae), truthful in your oracles, as has once been ordained, and may the unyielding order of events confirm it, link happy destinies to those already past...
'Do thou, O Luna, the constellations' Crescent Queen, to the maidens lend thine ear!...
'Then do ye, O deities, make teachable our youth and grant them virtuous ways; to the aged give tranquil peace...' (Horace, *Carmen Saeculare*.)

So long as these rites were duly accomplished, the Empire of the Romans remained intact... when, after Diocletian had abdicated the imperial power, the festival had been neglected, the Empire fell little by little into ruin... While Constantine and Licinius were already for the third time consuls, the term of one hundred and ten years fell due, and it was then necessary to celebrate the festival according to established custom; but as this was neglected, it was indeed fated that the situation should reach the catastrophic state which today overwhelms us [c.500]. (Zosimus, *Historia Nova*, II vii, 1.)

For Zosimus it is the non-celebration of the Games in 314 by the emperors favourable to Christianity which marks the beginning of the misfortunes of the Empire; the same opinion is found with Aurelius Victor in connection with the non-celebration of the one thousand one hundred years of Rome in 348. (Paschoud, Commentary on Zosimus, *Historia Nova*.)

[Palestinian]
The Virgin Mary

By the early Middle Ages May had five holy days of her own... The Church added one more for general observance, the feast of Our Lady Queen of Heaven, kept on 31st May... At the end of the 4th century the Virgin Mary received the same form of worship as that paid to the other Queens of Heaven. Epiphanius explains that the Collyridians worshipped Mary as Queen of Heaven... as a goddess, and thought she ought to be honoured and appeased with libations, oblations and offerings of cakes... the Collyridianae were women... who came from Thrace, and the yet more distant regions of Scythia, into Arabia. It was their practice to dress out a car, or a square throne, spread over it a linen cloth, and on a clear day once a year, place on it during the day a loaf of bread, or a cake, which they offered to the Virgin Mary. While they were pagans, they had been accustomed to bake and present to the goddess Venus, or Astarte, certain cakes which they called *collyrides*. And when they became Christians they thought this honour might now best be shown to Mary. (Ashe, *The Virgin*, pp150, 200.)

5 June
[Irish]
Domnu/St Gobnet/The Sheela-na-Gig

In the name of the female saint, Damhnaid, Damnata, Davnat or Dimna... we may possibly also recognize that of Domnu, Domna, or Damna... The celebrated centre of her worship was at Ballyvourney in Cork, where she was known, not as Davnat, but as Gobnet... the site of it is near the bank of the Sullane river. Here there is a green mound of slight elevation, 'Gobnatt's Stone'... The bushes on the mound were garnished with rags tied on by devotees, as is usual at sacred fountains.

Figure 54 Frog goddess, symbol of the vulva as opening to the Underworld. East European folk charm.

Near the cairn was the Holy Well, the branches over which were covered with rags. The ritual customary for the devotees consisted in going four times round the cairn and saying seven prayers at each round. The *Pattern*, or festival-day of Saint Gobnatt, was June 5th. The Boccoghs, or beggars, then assembled in great strength and exhibited a *sheela*... that is to say the image of a woman. [The female genitalia. Gyg is the name in Norse for a giantess, or perhaps one should say a goddess - Ed]. In the drawer of the sacristy at Ballyvourney was preserved a wooden image of Gobnatt, or Abigail, as she was called. The Boccoghs, whom Windele terms 'Irish Fakirs' were styled at Ballyvourney 'Gobnatt's Clergy'. It was said that they kept the image concealed, and only exhibited it on this occasion. (Borlase, *Dolmens* III, p1114.)

7 June
[Greek]

Athena

Callynteria and Plynteria (Feasts of Adorning and Cleansing) were the names given to the two chief days of a service of atonement held at Athens around May-June. The Erechtheum or sanctuary of Athena of the stronghold was cleansed; the ancient wooden image of the goddess was unclothed; the garments washed; and the image purified. These duties were performed with mysterious rites by the family of the Praxiegidae, with the aid of women called Plyntrides... (Seyffert, *Dictionary*.)

Figure 55   A Roman priestess in painted marble from the second century, perhaps a Vestal Virgin: British Museum.

[Roman]

Vesta

Curtained off from the rest of the main temple of Vesta was the *penus* which contained various sacred objects, but as none but the Vestals might enter it, their nature was never known, though widely guessed at. June 7th was the day of the opening of the *penus*, known as *Vesta aperit*. (OCD)

9 June
[Roman]

Vesta

The Vestalia, festivals in honour of Vesta, were observed at Rome on 9th June. Banquets were then prepared before the houses, and meat was sent to the Vestals to be offered to the gods, millstones were decked with garlands, and the asses that turned them were led round the city covered with garlands. (Lempriere, *Dictionary*.)

The matrons of the town walked barefooted in procession to her temple, to implore the blessing of the goddess for their households, and to make offerings to her in rude dishes, in remembrance of the time when the hearth served generally for the baking of bread. The millers and bakers also kept holiday. (Seyffert, *Dictionary*.)

'Oh Vesta, grant me thy favour! In thy service now I ope my lips, if it be lawful for me to come to thy holy rites. I was wrapt in prayer; I felt the heavenly deity and the glad ground gleamed with a purple light... they say that Rome had forty times celebrated the Parilia when the goddess, Guardian of Fire, was received in her temple; it was the work of that peaceful king (i.e. Numa).
'Something of olden custom has come down to our time: a clean platter contains the food offered to Vesta. Lo, loaves are hung on asses decked with wreaths, and flowery garlands veil the rough millstones... Hence the baker honours the hearth and the mistress of hearths and the she-ass that turns the mill-stones of pumice... work comes to a stop: the mills are empty and silent.' (Ovid, *Fasti* VI, p249.)

13 June
[Greek/Roman]

The Muses

The Nativity of the Muses. According to Hesiod the Muses are

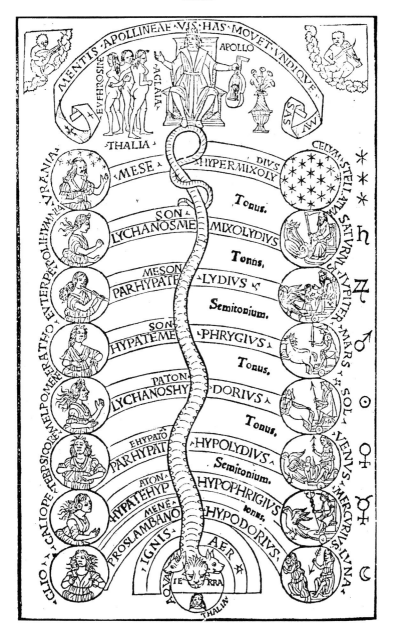

Figure 56 Apollo and the Nine Muses, goddesses of the Harmony of the Spheres. A woodcut from Franchino Gafori, Practica Musicae utriusque cantus *(1508).*

daughters of Mnemosyne (Memory), wife of Zeus, and are nine in number. Their names and attributes are: Calliope, she of the fair voice, epic song; Clio, she that extols, history; Euterpe, she that gladdens, lyric song; Thalia, she that flourishes, comedy; Melpomene, she that sings, tragedy; Terpsichore, she that rejoices in the dance, dancing; Erato, the lovely one, erotic poetry; Polyhymnia, she that is rich in hymns, sacred songs; Urania, astronomy [or the music of the spheres, the octave of eight notes taken together is the ninth Muse -Ed]. (Seyffert, *Dictionary*.)

15 June

[Roman]
Vesta

On June 15 the *penus* of the Temple of Vesta was closed, called *Vesta clud*. 'It is the day on which thou, O Tiber, dost send the sweepings of Vesta's temple down the Etruscan water to the sea.' (Ovid, *Fasti* VI, p713.)

'Necklaced asses suffice to make Her glad.' (Propertius, IV i, 21.)

CANCER

21 June

[Egyptian]

Wadjet

Wadjet, the Uraeus goddess, was regarded as governing the eleventh month of the Egyptian year.

[Roman]

Juno

The festival of Juno Moneta was held on the calends of June, and Juno was the great guardian of the female sex. (Brewer, *Dictionary*.)

Juno Luna

June coincides with a correlation by the Romans between Juno and the Moon, the goddess who confers menstruation on women. (Eisler, *The Royal Art of Astrology*, p212.)

[Greek]

All Heras/High Priestesses

Day of all *heras*. A *hera* is one who in the course of an earthly life has reached that single goal, achieving full communion with the Mother of all Things... A *hera* is often the guardian of a Temple, community or village. [A *hero* was the male equivalent: Heracles means 'beloved of Hera' -Ed] (*Lux Madriana Calendar, The Coming Age*, no. 15.)

[British]

The Great Mother

Stonehenge, that mysterious ancient construction of sarsen stones, linked together for aeons like a circle of Greek dancers, alone in the middle of a desolate and uninhabited plain, is the setting for the modern

Figure 57   Stonehenge on Summer Solstice morning 1987 as the rays of the sun enter the womb of the temple sanctum: kind permission of The Times.

Druids' solstice ceremonies. The words are spoken, perhaps a prayer or invocation to the Great Mother... Water is also blessed in the name of the Great Mother so that the link between Earth and Mankind may also be renewed and strengthened. (Green, *A Harvest of Festivals*, p78.)

On Midsummer's Day the sun's rays, beaming from above the heel (Helios) stone, flash down the pathway leading into the centre of the Temple, marking the beginning of Time for another year. (-Ed)

23 June

[Mesopotamian]

Inanna/Ishtar/Isis/Venus

The rites of Ishtar and Tammuz were in the Middle East originally celebrated at midsummer, at the time Sirius rose in Leo after a disappearance of seventy days. For countries further north the celebrations were in later history transposed to the Vernal equinox. To underline the dramatic continuity of the cult we have for comparison's sake in this calendar placed the middle eastern material with the European, in March. For those still living in the Middle East, however, it would be appropriate still to celebrate the Isis/Osiris or Ishtar/Tammuz festivals in the month of Tammuz, still corresponding to June/July in the moveable calendar of the Jews. -Ed

[British]
The Great Goddess

In Cornwall the people of Helston flock to Manhay Farm in the old parish of Wendron, where, as darkness falls, a great bonfire will be kindled. This will be but one in a chain of beacons throughout the eighty-odd miles of the Cornish peninsula, a living strand of fire stretching from Chael Carn Berea near Land's End, to Kit Hill near the Devon border.

The Midsummer Eve Bonfire celebrations were revived in 1929 by the Federation of Old Cornwall Societies, which has been responsible for the rescue and maintenance of many of Cornwall's lapsed customs... The prayer for the Benediction of the Bonfire is spoken first in English, then in Cornish close to the original language of the old Celtic Sun-worshippers... The pagan theme is underlined by the next participant, the Lady of the Flowers. Whether young, middle-aged or elderly, whether costumed or in ordinary clothes, she is obviously representative of the Earth Mother, the Great Goddess who shared with the deities of Sun and Moon and Sea the homage of the ancient peoples. Bearing her beribboned sheaf of flowers and herbs, she steps forward to the unlit stack. Once the sacrificial bouquet has been tossed on to its woody altar, the long-awaited moment of kindling is at hand. (Green, *A Harvest of Festivals*, p139.)

The season at which these fire-festivals have been most generally held all over Europe is the Summer Solstice, that is Midsummer Eve (23 June) or Midsummer Day (24 June). We cannot doubt that the celebration dates from a time long before the beginning of our era. Whatever their origin, they have prevailed all over this quarter of the globe, from Ireland on the West to Russia on the East, and from Norway and Sweden on the North to Spain and Greece on the South. According to a mediaeval writer, the three great features of the Midsummer celebration were the bonfires, the procession with torches round the fields, and the custom of rolling a wheel — and he explains the custom of trundling a wheel to mean that the sun, having now reached the highest point in the ecliptic, begins thenceforward to descend. (Frazer, *The Golden Bough*, abgd, p622.)

[North African]
Fatimah

The custom of kindling bonfires on Midsummer Day or on Midsummer Eve is widely spread among Mohammedan peoples of North Africa, particularly in Morocco and Algeria... The celebration of the midsummer festival by these peoples is particularly remarkable, because the Muslim Calendar, being purely lunar and uncorrected by intercalation, necessarily takes no note of festivals which occupy fixed points in the

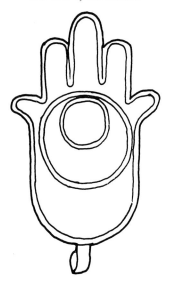

Figure 58   The Hand of Fatima, a Muslim Goddess symbol from North Africa. The five fingers refer to the five 'Pillars of Islam', the five-foldness signifying Venus, and this hand holds in its palm the sun and moon also. Muslims' day of worship is Friday, Venus's day (see also Figures 23 and 59).

solar year. This fact of itself seems to prove that among the Muslims of Northern Africa, as among the Christian peoples of Europe, the Midsummer festival is quite independent of the religion which the people publicly profess, and is the relic of a far older paganism. (Frazer, *The Golden Bough* abgd, p631.)

24 June

[Scandinavian]

The Midsummer Bride

In Sweden the ceremonies associated elsewhere with May Day or Whitsuntide commonly take place at Midsummer. Accordingly we find that in some parts of the Swedish province of Blekinge they still choose a Midsummer Bride to whom the church coronet is occasionally lent. The girl selects for herself a Bridegroom, and a collection is made for the pair, who for the time being are looked on as man and wife. The other youths also choose each his bride. A similar ceremony seems to still be kept up in Norway. (Frazer, *The Golden Bough*, abgd, p131.)

2 July

[Palestinian]

St Elizabeth and The Virgin Mary

The feast of Our Lady's Visitation was instituted by Urban VII in the 14C... In 1441 the feast was confirmed by the Council of Basel, and fixed for 2nd July. (Bridgett, *Our Lady's Dowry*, p235.)

And Mary arose in those days, and went into the hill country with haste, into a city of Judah;

And entered into the house of Zacharias, and saluted Elizabeth...

And Mary abode with her about three months, and returned to her own house. (Luke i, 39)

Now she was sixteen years old. (James xii, 2)

On the feast of the Visitation of the Blessed Virgin, 1499, Andrew Lyall, Treasurer of the Cathedral in Aberdeen made a present of a large silver statue of our Lady of Pity, weighing 120 ounces, to the high altar. Thereupon William the Bishop made an ordinance that this statue should be carried in procession round the Cathedral on all the solemn feasts of the Glorious Virgin, and granted forty days' indulgence to all who should devoutly follow in the procession. (*Aberdeen Registers.*)

8 July

[Graeco-Egyptian]

Arsinoe

Arsinoe II, sister and wife of Ptolemy II Philadelphus was worshipped under the name of Venus Zephyritis. Dinochares began to build her a temple with lodestones, in which there stood a statue of Arsinoe suspended in the air. (Lempriere, *Dictionary.*)

The poet Callimachus states that an altar and a holy enclosure were established in her honour near the Emporium and in a fragment addresses her, 'O bride, already up under the stars of the Wain'.

10 July

[English]

Lady Godiva

Historians give Leofrick, Duke of Mercia a great Character; but especially they extoll Godiva his Wife... 'Tis related of this Lady that in order to free the inhabitants of Coventry from a heavy Tax laid on them by her Husband she readily consented to perform a very extraordinary Act. The Earl, upon her interceding in their Behalf, told her, he wou'd ease them of their Burden, provided she wou'd ride on Horseback naked, from one End of the Town to the other. This condition gave the Burghers but little Hopes of being reliev'd. But Godiva undertook the Matter, covering her Body with her Hair... there is a Procession or cavalcade still made there every Year in memory of Godiva, with a Figure representing a naked Woman riding thro' the City.' (De Rapin Thoyras, *History of England* II, p80.)

In the Lady Godiva procession of Southam, two figures were carried, one white and one black, the Goddess as Holda and Hel... What seems to have happened is that after the Conquest the monks disguised a local May-eve procession of the Goddess Goda which always falls on a Friday, the Goddess's own day. (Graves, *The White Goddess*, p405.)

11 July
[South Italian]
Theano

Theano, wife of Pythagoras was said to be a native of Crotona or Crete. (Lempriere, *Dictionary*.)

'The second model shall be the famous Theano... Theano shall contribute the greatness of her intellect.'

16 July
[Palestinian]
Mary, Flower of Carmel

Commemoration of the Blessed Virgin Mary of Mount Carmel: the Carmelite Order, which held the Virgin Mary in special reverence ... allotted Her no fewer than twenty-three days of its calendar. (Ashe, *The Virgin*.)

[The flower has many levels of symbolism, one being the star. As this festival marks the time Sirius rises (in Graeco-Egyptian times it would have been 19/20 July) it is likely the Flower of Carmel represents Mary as Sirius. -Ed]

Rosa

The Romans were extravagantly fond of roses and used them especially on all manner of festival occasions... It is therefore not remarkable

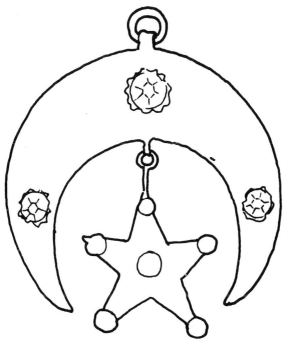

Figure 59 Another North African Muslim woman's pendant showing the star of Sirius/Venus within the crescent moon of Luna.

that a feast of roses, the Rosalia, was a common event. Feasts of roses are recorded in a number of documents on dates ranging from about 1st June to the middle of July — in other words, at the time of year when roses were to be had abundantly. (Guirand and Pierre, *New Larousse*, p210.)

The rose was especially sacred to Venus, as goddess of love. (Waite, *The Brotherhood of the Rosy Cross*, p85.)

Rosa Mundi

On this joyous summer festival we celebrate the Rose of the World, the Heart of Creation; the Consuming Fire. It is supremely the Mother's festival, and is the time that we meditate most deeply upon our relationship to Her. She is the Maker and Shaper of each individual soul in its pure and perfect form. We are born from Her joy, and only in Her are we whole.

It is the custom at the Rosa Mundi rite for the handmaid to give everyone a rose to hold during the contemplation, that they may meditate upon the inner meaning of the manifest flower. The altar is decked with roses and candles. (*The Coming Age*, p15.)

The Rose, the grandest, the noblest of Nature's symbols. To the Rosicrucian the Rose was the symbol of Nature, of the ever prolific and virgin Earth, considered as feminine and represented as a virgin woman by the Egyptian initiates, of Isis, the mother and nourisher of man. (Blavatsky, *The Secret Doctrine*, V, p292.)

19 July
Great Panathenaia — Day One of Six Days
[Egyptian]
Mut

Every year in the month of Paophi, the second month of the floods, came the period of eleven days during which the capital celebrated the feast of Opet... Amun and his spouse Mut (the Karnak form of Isis), accompanied by the god Khonsu, proceeded ceremonially at the time of this 'divine emergence', giving the crowd a glimpse of the triad of its three great gods. With the return of the royal family (of Tutankhamun) to Thebes, the feast of Opet recovered its lustre, and

Figure 60 The present-day Muslim ornaments of Figures 58 and 59 refer precisely to the same astronomical measures contained in the 'well-tempered year' as were celebrated at the Feast of Opet. Here Isis (Sirius/Venus) presents the Pharaoh Seti I as a personification of her child Khonsu (the boy moon-god) to her spouse Amun, lord of the sky and the sun's annual course. Nineteenth dynasty, Karnak, Thebes.

the majestic and festive spectacle it provided on the banks of the Nile and round the temples so impressed Tutankhamun that he had all its phases sculpted [on the walls of the temple of Luxor]. (Desroches-Noblecourt, *Tutankamen*, p185.)

[The tell-tale number, eleven, points to the festival being the period of 'catching up' the lunar year to the solar by the intercalation of that many days to close the eleven-day discrepancy between lunar and solar years. This would originally have been a festival to mark time before the rising of Sirius and the inauguration of the New Year. Today the lunar Muslim Feast of Ramadan falls behind in date by eleven days each year, and takes thirty-three years to come round to the same solar starting point from which it originally began. -Ed]

Sothis

It must have been early recognized that the Nile began to rise afresh about the same time that the brilliant star Sirius ('the Dog Star'), after having been invisible for a prolonged period, was first again observed in the sky shortly before sunrise. Consequently this latter event, described by modern astronomers as the heliacal rising of Sirius, and by the ancient Egyptians as *prt Spdt* ('the going out of (the goddess) Sothis') came to be regarded as the true New Year's Day (*wpt-rnpt*, 'opening of the year'), i.e. 'first month of inundation, day 1'. (Gardiner, *Egyptian Grammar*, p205.)

The Dog Days were those days around the heliacal rising of the Dog Star, noted from ancient times as the hottest period of the year in the Northern hemisphere... their duration has been reckoned as from 30 to 54 days. A generally accepted period is from July 3 to August 15. (*Whitaker's Almanac*.)

[Greek]

Athena

The Panathenaia took place in July at the height of the summer heat, when the need for rain was the greatest. But the month Hecatombaion, in which it was celebrated, was the first month of the Athenian year and the day of the festival was the birthday of the goddess. When the goddess became a war-goddess, it was fabled that she was born on Olympus... But... the day of her birth was... the day of the beginning of the new year, with its returning life. (Harrison, *Art and Ritual*, p182.)

According to Hesiod's *Theogony*, p886, Athena is the daughter of Metis, the first wife of Zeus.

From the time of Pisistratus, the Great Panathenaea was held every fifth year, in the third year of every Olympia, from the 24th to 29th of Hecatombaeon. (Seyffert, *Dictionary*.)

Figure 61 The two leading goddesses of Greece, Hera, consort of Zeus, and Athena, born from his head, on a decree stela from Athens of 405 BC: Athens Museum.

[Romano-Egyptian]
Aphrodite

At Alexandria the Rites consisted of a magnificent pageant of the wedding of Adonis and Aphrodite... There was, perhaps, considerable variation in the content as in the date of the festival... In fifth-century Athens they were held in April, in Ptolemaic Egypt perhaps in September, while under the Empire the accepted date was 19th July. (*OCD*)

20 July

Great Panathenaia — Day Two of Six Days

[Syrian]
St Margaret of Antioch

The Orientals pay reverence to her by the name of St Pelagia or St Marina, and the western church by that of St Geruma or St Margaret. She was born in the second half of the third century. (*Encyclopaedia Britannica*, 1810 edn.)

LEO

21 July

Great Panathenaia — Day Three of Six Days

Nana

Nana on the lioness, a form of Kybele, appears in the ancient art of India, Mesopotamia and the Ancient Middle East from 3000 BC up to Classical times and beyond, and is a blend of the sign of Virgo with Leo. [Ed]

[South Italian]

Damo

Daughter of Pythagoras and Theano. At his death Pythagoras entrusted her with all the secrets of his philosophy, and gave her the unlimited care of his compositions. (Lempriere, *Dictionary*.)

22 July

Great Panathenaia — Day Four of Six Days

[Palestinian]

St Mary Magdalene

Perhaps the Magdalene — that elusive woman in the Gospels — was in fact Jesus' wife...

Popular tradition notwithstanding, the Magdalene is not, at any point in any of the Gospels, said to be a prostitute. When she is first mentioned in the Gospel of Luke, she is described as a woman 'out of whom

Figure 62 Clay goddess seated on her lioness throne (restored), found at Catal Huyuk, Turkey and dating to the seventh millennium BC: Ankara Museum. A similar example from the same museum shows her giving birth to the Bull of the Year.

went seven devils'. It is generally assumed that this phrase refers to a species of exorcism on Jesus' part, implying the Magdalene was possessed. But the phrase may equally refer to some sort of conversion and/or ritual initiation. The cult of Ishtar or Astarte — the Mother Goddess and 'Queen of Heaven' — involved, for example, a seven-stage initiation. Prior to her affiliation with Jesus, the Magdalene may well have been associated with such a cult. Migdala, or Magdala, was 'the Village of Doves', and there is some evidence that sacrificial doves were in fact bred there. And the dove was the sacred symbol of Astarte...

The whole episode of Jesus' anointing would seem to be an affair of

considerable consequence. Why else would it be emphasised by the
Gospels to the extent it is?... One must remember that anointing was
the traditional prerogative of kings — and of the 'rightful Messiah',
which means 'the anointed one'. From this, it follows that Jesus becomes
an authentic Messiah by virtue of his anointing. And the woman who
consecrates him in that august role can hardly be unimportant. (Baigent
et al. *The Holy Blood and The Holy Grail.*)

23 July

Great Panathenaia — Day Five of Six Days

Athena

The Panathenaea, festivals in honour of the patroness of Athens, were
first instituted by Erechtheus or Orpheus and called Athenaea, but
Theseus afterwards renewed them... In the first years of the institution,
they were observed only one day, but afterwards the time was prolonged, and the celebration was attended with greater pomp and solemnity. The festivals were two; the Great Panathenaea which was observed
every fifth year beginning on the 22nd of Hecatombeion, and the Lesser
Panathenaea which were kept every third year, or rather annually,
beginning on the 21st or 20th of Thargelion [for which see under 19
March].
[Note again that the Great Panathenaea, being on a five-yearly cycle,
clearly served to mark the Venus synodic period. The 'weaving of the
peplos' was a symbolic analogue of the patterns woven by Venus over
its eight revolutions round the earth within five earth years. The figure
eight was equally, in the form of Her Shield, a potent symbol of the
Goddess, and an allusion to the Venus/Earth relationship. -Ed]
   Four Arrhephoroi, or young virgins between seven and eleven years
of age were yearly chosen from the houses of noble citizens and had
to spend several months at the temple of Athena in the Acropolis and
take part in its services. Two of them had the task of commencing the
cloak or shawl which the women of Athens wove and presented to the
Goddess at the Panathenaea. The other two on the night of the festival
received from the priestess of Athena certain coffers with unknown contents, which they carried in procession on their heads to a natural grotto
beside the temple of Aphrodite of the gardens, receiving something
equally mysterious in exchange, which they carried to the temple on
the Acropolis. ...The grand procession carried through the city the costly
embroidered, saffron coloured garment, the Peplos. (Seyffert, *Dictionary.*)
Athena's Peplos was of a white colour, without sleeves, and embroidered
with gold. Upon it were described the achievements of the Goddess.
In the procession of the Peplos, there was an engine built in the form

Figure 63 The figure of eight shield of Athena can be traced back to the shield and crossed arrows of Neith of Sais, Egypt, shown here on the royal stela of the Lady Meryt of the second dynasty: Cairo Museum.

Figure 64 The young Athenian girls who have woven the new peplos for the cult image of Athena present it to the Archon of Athens, while Athena and her consort Hephaistos look on. This panel of the fifth century BC Parthenon Frieze would have appeared directly over the doorway leading into the sanctuary which housed the chryselephantine statue of Athena: British Museum.

of a ship upon which Athena's garment was hung as a sail, and the whole was conducted to the citadel, where the Peplos was placed upon Athena's statue, which was laid upon a bed woven or strewed with flowers. (Lempriere, *Dictionary*.)

24th July
Great Panathenaia — Day Six of Six Days
[Egyptian]
Neith/Athena

A feast of lamps was also celebrated at Sais in Egypt in honour of Isis-Neith. The ceremony took place in an under-chapel beneath the Temple. Lamps were carried in procession around the coffin of Osiris. (Harding, *Women's Mysteries*, p130.)

'There is a third great festival in Sais to Athena.' (Herodotos, II, 59) 'For they often times call Isis by the name of Athena.' (Plutarch, *De Iside et Osiride*, 376A.)

'In Sais the statue of Athena, whom they believe to be Isis, bore the inscription: "I am all that has been and is and shall be, and none mortal hath lifted my Veil"' (Plutarch, *De Iside et Osiride*, 354C.)

In one of the Hermetic texts called *Peplos* (The Veil) it is said that the Veil 'signified the Veil of the Universe, studded with stars, the many-coloured Veil of Nature, the famous Veil or Robe of Isis, that no mortal has raised'. (Harding, *Women's Mysteries*, p237.)

To raise the Veil of Isis must mean to see Nature as she really is, to understand what it is that underlies the manifestations of this world, and of the emotions which so move us, to see them in their ultimate reality, not veiled any longer... S(he) who is able to do that and so to face reality becomes consciously immortal... conscious of immortality. (Mead, *Thrice-Greatest Hermes* I, p62.)

25 July
[Roman]
Salacia

A Roman goddess of salt water, identified with the Greek Amphitrite, and regarded as the wife of Neptune... His festival is of the oldest series;

we know concerning its ritual only that arbours (umbrae) of boughs were commonly erected... it may be conjectured that its object was to obtain sufficient water at this hot and dry time of year. (*OCD*)

26 July

[Palestinian]

St Anne

Festival of St Anne, Mother of the Virgin Mary, a saint particularly venerated by the Knights Templar.

27 July

[Egyptian]

Hatshepsut, Queen of Egypt

A Queen-Priestess, the only ruling female Pharaoh of Egypt, who fostered exploration and the arts, and during her lifetime cultivated government by peaceful means.

28 July

[Greek]

Pythias

The mother of Pythagoras, from her name she is likely to have officiated at Delphi at the Pythian oracle.

29 July

[Palestinian]

St Martha

Martha, devoted to Jesus in company with her sister Mary, served by actions rather than words.

Figure 65   A painted limestone sculpture of Queen and High Priestess Hatshepsut of the eighteenth dynasty as a sphinx who has conquered Time: Cairo Museum.

31 July
Lammas Eve
[Russian]
Helena Blavatsky (1831-91)

Abandoning a marriage of three months' duration, the youthful Mme Blavatsky travelled widely in Asia, South America, Africa and India,

Figure 66   A snake priestess and healer on a seal design from archaic Cyprus.

and acted as a pathfinder to others in her search for the perennial philosophy beyond all religions. Believing in 'the Universal Brotherhood of Man', in 1875 she founded the Theosophical Society. Her two books, *Isis Unveiled* (1877) and *The Secret Doctrine* (1888), if now with the benefit of more accurate information seeming verbose and sometimes inaccurate, are remarkable syntheses, for her time, of the key traditions of sacred knowledge. She was a pioneer in the Western rediscovery of the Goddesses that preceded the Virgin Mary.

1 August

[Greek]

Demeter and Ceres

The festivals of late summer open the great Mysteries of Life, a cycle

Figure 67   Demeter and Persephone with torch and staff guide the soul in its quest,
symbolized by the young Ptolemaeus. A votive relief from Eleusis, fifth century BC:
Athens Museum.

which spans a quarter of the year. They celebrate the Goddess as the
Source of all life, the Creatrix and Sustainer of the cycles of existence
through which the soul moves. The ultimate revolution in the life of
every soul, turning back to the Goddess is particularly a subject for
meditation during the late summer and autumn. The symbol of the

Festival of Regeneration is the ear of corn. This festival is concerned with the movement between lives and the resurgence of new life, celebrating the Mother of our rebirth and the Daughter as Our Lady of the Dark Gates, She who guards and guides all souls in the transition from one life to the next. (*The Coming Age*, no.11.)

[European]
The Earth Goddess

Lammas, or Lughnasad, the Celtic festival of the beginning of Autumn... is the festival marking the transformation of the Goddess into her Earth Mother aspect, and it seems likely, as with the Tailltean Fair, that the sites most sacred at this time of the cycle were the mounds of the Earth Goddess... The community reflected on the reality that the Mother aspect of the Goddess, having come to fruition, from Lammas on would enter the Earth and slowly become transformed into the Old Woman-Hecate-Cailleach aspect which would emerge at Samhain. (McLean, *Fire Festivals*, pp20-22.)

The August or Harvest Games, were held in honour of Lugh in ancient times, even on the Continent, especially at Lyons. (Dineen, *Dictionary*.)

[Irish]
Carman

The people of Leinster held a provincial Fair at Carman or Wexford once every three years, which began on Lughnasad... they were promised various blessings - plenty and prosperity, corn, milk, fruit... and freedom from subjection to any other province. Women played a conspicuous part in this fair and had councils of their own to discuss those subjects specially pertaining to women. (Joyce, *Social History of Ireland* II, p441.)

Carman and her three sons came from Athens to Wexford (Borlase, *Dolmens* III, p829.)

Carman, in whose honour a seasonal festival was established, exhibits to a marked degree the concept of the magical powers of the female as opposed to the physical force employed by the male. (Ross, *Pagan Celtic Britain*, p226.)

Macha, Queen of Ireland

In the Dinnsenchus, as well as in other authorities, we are told that the Annual Fair of Macha held at Armagh was established to commemorate Queen Macha of the Golden Hair, who had founded the palace there. ...The Machas likewise were associated with this feast: The Three Machas are, according to Irish literary tradition, Macha wife of

Nemed, Macha wife of Crunnchu and Macha the Red. The third Macha, of the Red, or Golden, Hair reigned as Queen of Ireland c.377 BC. (Joyce, *Social History of Ireland* II, p435.)

Tailte

Prince Lughnaidh the Long-Handed first ordained the assembly of Tailtean in honour of the memory of the Princess Tailte, who had taken care of his education in his minority and had him instructed in the maxims of government and accomplished him in polite learning. In gratitude he instituted the assembly and appointed tilts and tournaments as tribute to her memory. Those warlike exercises resembled the old Olympic games, and were observed upon the first of August every year, a day which is still distinguished by the name of Lughnasa. (Keating, *General History of Ireland*, pp93, 235.)

Tailte was a chieftainess of the Fir Bolg, foster-mother of Lugh. At her assembly hurling matches were held and marriage contracts were signed. (Dinneen, *Dictionary*.)

Lammas or Lughnasad, the Celtic festival of the beginning of Autumn, is recorded as being established by the Celtic God of light, Lugh, in honour of his foster mother, the Earth Goddess Tailte. (McLean, *Fire Festivals*, p20.)

Lammas is a day for baking bread in celebration of the first fruits of the wheat harvest. (*Druids Calendar*.)

[British]
Blodeuwedd

In some places at midsummer, but more properly at Lughnasadh, it was the custom to make a great bonfire on some high hilltop and to heat in it a wheel, which was normally a heavy oaken wagon-wheel. When this was glowing red within its metal tyre, it was bowled down the hilltop eagerly watched by the community, who drew from its course auguries for the coming season. The true significance of the fiery wheel was to symbolize the descent of the sun from its midsummer height. Besides this ritual, the festival of Lughnasadh was associated with the myth of the marriage of Lugh to Blodeuwedd, who was one of the loveliest forms of the Earth-Goddess. (Denning and Phillips, *The Magical Philosophy* II, p42.)

12 August
[Italian]

St Claire

Born at Assisi in 1193, the Shakti of St Francis, she was canonized by

Pope Alexander IV in 1255. (*Irish Catholic Directory.*)

13 August
[Greece]

Hecate

On 13th August there was a great festival of Hecate the Moon Goddess in Greece, and of Diana, her direct descendant, in Rome, for the harvest ripens earlier in these southern countries than it does farther north. On this day the Goddess's aid was invoked to avert storms which might injure the coming harvest. This festival was continued by the Catholic Church. The date of 15 August was chosen for celebrating the feast of the Assumption of the Blessed Virgin. The connection between the pagan and the Christian ceremony is a very interesting one. The special feature of the Christian festival centres round prayers addressed to the Virgin Mary as they formerly were to the moon goddesses who preceded her, to turn aside storms until the fields are reaped of their fruits. There is a passage in the Syriac text of *The Departure of My Lady Mary from this World* which runs thus:

> And the apostles also ordered that there should be a commemoration of the Blessed One on the thirteenth Ab (August), on account of the vines bearing bunches of grapes and on account of the trees bearing fruit, that clouds of hail, bearing stones of wrath, might not come, and the trees be broken, and the vines with their clusters.
>
> (Harding, *Women's Mysteries*, p109.)

15 August
[Roman]

Diana

Her chief festival was called the Festival of Torches, celebrated on 15 August. Her groves shone with a multitude of torches. (Harding, *Women's Mysteries*, p130.)

[Palestinian]

The Virgin Mary

The Virgin Mary was taken to heaven in the year 45 AD in her corporeal form, being at the time seventy-five years of age. (Brewer, *Dictionary.*)

Figure 68 St Thomas reaches out for his life-line, the red girdle of the Virgin of
Heaven, as depicted by the fifteenth century Italian painter, Matteo: courtesy The
Trustees of the National Gallery, London. (See also Figure 92.)

The Jerusalem date of 15th August was made obligatory by the Emperor Maurice about 600 AD, and it became general in the West towards 650 AD. (Ashe, *The Virgin*, p200.)

'Then Thomas told them... how he had been brought to the Mount of Olives and seen the ascension of Mary and she had given him her girdle: and he showed it.' (*Apocryphal New Testament*, p218.)

Hokmah, Sophia, The Holy Wisdom

Under a compulsion that was never discussed, the two Marian dogmas (i.e. the Immaculate Conception and the Assumption) drew Wisdom into the Liturgy of their feast-days... Almost casually Mary was conceded the Jewish demigoddess's attributes... The siting of several of her churches on ground sacred to Athena was a continuity. It evoked not only the pagan wisdom-goddess but others connected with her. The Greek Church dallied with the Mary-Wisdom equation... Russian churches of the same name (Sancta Sophia), at Kiev and Novgorod for instance, applied it to Mary and expressed that idea in their icons. They held their 'Feasts of Title' on Marian days. Orthodox Russia instituted a special Mass combining the Holy Wisdom with the Assumption. (Ashe, *The Virgin*, p213.)

19 August

[Roman]

Venus and Minerva

'The 19th of August was called the Country V*inalia* because at that time a temple was dedicated to Venus and gardens were set apart for her, and then the kitchen-gardeners went on holiday. Since, as we are told, the deities help those who call upon them, I will first invoke them... I beseech Minerva and Venus, of whom the one protects the oliveyard, and the other the garden and in her honour the rustic Vinalia has been established.' (Varro.)

VIRGO

21 August

[Mesopotamian]

Inanna

Among the Sumerians Inanna was already the grain goddess, and both correspond astronomically and astrologically to the virgin with the ear of grain. (Neumann, *The Great Mother*, p287.)

Beltis

In Assyria Virgo represented Beltis as the star Spica in Virgo. (Allen, *Star Names*, p468.)

Ishtar

Ishtar, the Queen of the Stars, was the Ashtoreth of the Book of Kings (xi,5,33)... Astarte of Syria, the last philologically akin to our Esther and Star, the Greek Aster. (Allen, *Star Names*, p463.)

[Egyptian]

Isis

Eratosthenes and Avienus identified Virgo with Isis, the thousand-named goddess, holding the wheat-ears in her hand that she afterwards dropped to form the Milky Way, or clasping in her hands the young Horus. (Allen, *Star Names*, p462.)

[Greek]

Parthenos

Beneath both feet of Bootes mark the Maiden (Parthenos), who in her hands bears the gleaming Ear of Corn. (Aratus, *Phaenomena*, p95.)

'We shall also set forth for ready use a list of several nations which

Figure 69   A fragment of a basalt vase dedicated by the people's leader, Entemena of Lagash, Mesopotamia, c. 2450 BC, shows Inanna, the primordial Virgo, with feather and bull-crescent crown, wheat sprouting from her shoulders and a cluster of dates in one hand: Berlin Museum.

are in familiarity [with Virgo]... Mesopotamia, Babylonia, Assyria, Hellas, Achaia, Crete.' (Ptolemy, *Tetrabiblos* II,3.)

Kore

Virgo was known in the Attic dialect as Kore, the Maiden... while in the Ionic dialect she was called *Spicifera Virgo Cereres*, The Wheat-Bearing Maiden. (Allen, *Star Names*, p460.)

[Palestinian]
The Virgin Mary

In modern representations, Virgo being also the symbol of the Virgin Mary, the lily takes the place of the corn and poppies.

[Irish]
The Virgin Mary

On 21 August 1879 fifteen people of various ages saw Mary wearing a white dress and crown at Cnoc Mhuire. Later, on the Hill of Mary at Cnoc Mhuire in October 1979, Pope John Paul II addressed Mary as 'Queen of Ireland'.

22 August

[Irish]

The Virgin Mary

On the Octave of the Feast of the Assumption, the Immaculate Heart of the Blessed Virgin Mary is celebrated.

Figure 70 A present-day Muslim woman's pendant shows the star of Venus interspersed with her vulvas.

23 August

[Greek]

Moira

This day is dedicated to the Genia of Personal Fate. The threads of Moira draw all things in life together. Her particular symbols are the wheel and the scales. This day is especially one for examining the direction of one's soul and making resolutions for the future. (*The Coming Age*, no.11.)

Nemesis

The Greeks celebrated a festival called the Nemesia in memory of deceased persons, as the goddess Nemesis was supposed to defend the relics and memory of the dead from all insult. (Lempriere, *Dictionary*.)

25 August

[Roman]

Ops

Ops, meaning Abundance, was the old Italian goddess of fertility. As goddess of sowing and reaping she had on this day, under the name of Consivia, a special festival, the Opeconsiva, which only the Vestals and one of the *pontifices* could attend because her shrine in the Regia was so tiny. As her abode was in the earth, her worshippers invoked her while seated and touching the ground. (Seyffert, *Dictionary*, based on Macrobius and Varro.)

26 August

[Finnish]

Ilmatar

Ilmatar, also known as Luonnotar, or the Water Mother, was the Creatrix of the World. Upon her knees the duck laid the six golden eggs and the one iron egg from which the world was made. (Catherine Koppana, *unpubl. MS on Finnish Festivals*.)

29 August

[Egyptian]

Hathor

New Year of the fixed Alexandrian Calendar, Thoth 1: Great Festivals were celebrated in the temple of Denderah, above all on New Year's day, which was the anniversary of her birth. Before dawn the priestesses would bring Hathor's image out onto the terrace to expose it to the rays of the rising sun. The rejoicing that followed was a pretext for a veritable carnival, and the day ended in song and intoxication. (Ions, *Egyptian Mythology*, p79.)

The gods of heaven exclaim 'Ah!' in satisfaction, the inhabitants of the earth are full of gladness, the Hathors beat their tabors, the great ladies wave their mystic whips, all those who are gathered together in the town are drunk with wine and crowned with flowers; the tradespeople of the place walk joyously about, their heads scented with perfumed oils, all the children rejoice in honour of the goddess, from the rising to the setting of the sun. (Dumichen, *Dendera*, quoted Maspero, *Dawn of Civilisation*, p322.)

Figure 71   Hathor, Goddess of earthly love, music and pleasure, is sometimes portrayed, as on this third century BC column capital, by a maiden with cow-ears and hair studded with roses: Louvre, Réunion des Musées Nationaux.

8 September

[Palestinian]
The Virgin Mary and her Mother, St Anne

The Nativity of the Blessed Virgin Mary. In Coptic and other lives of the Virgin she was born on 15th of Hathor. (*Apocryphal New Testament*, p87.)

'And her months were fulfilled, and in the ninth month Anna brought forth, and she said unto the midwife: What have I brought forth? And she said: a female. And Anna said, My soul is magnified this day... and she gave suck to the child and called her name Mary.' (*The Book of St James (The Protoevangelium)*, V, 2.)

Mary's Nativity was added to the Calendar between 650 and 700. (Ashe, *The Virgin*, p200.)

[Saxon]

The fourth feast celebrated by the Anglo-Saxons was that of Our Lady's Nativity... A poem of St Aldhelm, who wrote in the seventh century in England, distinctly states that the feast of the dedication of the church built by the Princess Bugge was the Nativity of our Lady.

The festival is also mentioned by The Venerable Bede, who died in 735. Butler gives us authorities which prove its celebration in Rome in the sixth century. In the ninth and tenth centuries it was celebrated in many places with great pomp, and ranked as one of the principal festivals of the Church. Pope Innocent IV in 1243 ordered that an Octave should be kept. (Bridgett, *Our Lady's Dowry*, p228.)

9 September

[Greek]

Asclepigenaia

An Eleusinian Priestess. (*Perpetual Festival Calendar*.)

11 September

[Egyptian]
The Matriarchy of Egypt

All Queens were High Priestesses of Egypt, and Initiates of the Inner Mysteries. (*Perpetual Festival Calendar*.)

Their power was hidden, but it was they who ruled Egypt through the Pharoah of the time, whether he was their brother, husband or father. No man could become Pharoah (the Living Horus, the resurrected Osiris) other than by marriage to such a Lady of the Royal Line which ran through the female side, and derived ultimately from Isis. (-Ed)

12 September
[Greek]
Astraea

'But another tale is current among men, how of old she (Parthenos) dwelt on earth and met men face to face, nor ever disdained in olden time the tribes of men and women, but mingling with them took her seat, immortal though she was. Her men called Justice (Dike)... Nor yet in that age had men knowledge of hateful strife... Even so long as the earth nurtured the Golden Age, she had her dwelling on earth... Yet in that Silver Age was she still upon the earth, but from the echoing hills at eventide she came alone. But when they, too, were dead, and when, more ruinous than they which went before, the Race of Bronze was born, who were the first to forge the sword of the highwayman, and the first to eat the flesh of the ploughing-ox, then verily did Justice loathe that race of men and fly heavenward and took up that abode, where even now in the night-time the Maiden (Virgo) is seen of men, established near to far-seen Bootes.' (Aratus, *Phaenomena*, p98.)

The Sibylline Books, supposed to record the utterances of the famous Sibyl of Cumae, contained the prophecy of a new circuit of the Ages after the Age of Iron had passed. (Fairclough (ed.), *Virgil* I, p29.)

'Now is come the last age of the Song of Cumae; the great line of the centuries begins anew. Now the Virgin returns... Now a new generation descends from heaven on high... and a golden race springs up throughout the world!' (Virgil, *Eclogues*, iv.)

[Palestinian]
The Virgin Mary

The Most Holy Name of Mary is celebrated on 12 September by the Carmelite Order. (Ashe, *The Virgin*, p201.)

17 September

[German]

Hildegard of Bingen

Educated in the Celtic Christian tradition by Jutta, a holy anchoress, at the age of eight Hildegard had joined a monastery housing both monks and nuns, as was usual in the Celtic church. During her life (1098-1179) she wrote over a hundred letters to emperors, popes, bishops, archbishops, nuns and the nobility, as well as seventy poems and nine books describing her visions of the universe, dictated to her secretary, Monk Volmar, and for which she had special miniatures painted under her instruction.

In her own words, 'When I was forty-two years and seven months old, a burning light of tremendous brightness coming from heaven poured into my entire mind. Like a flame that does not burn but enkindles, it inflamed my entire heart and my entire breast, just like the sun that warms an object with its rays... All of a sudden, I was able to taste of the understanding of the narration of books. I saw the psalter clearly and the evangelists and other Catholic books of the Old and New Testaments.'

In a letter to Abbot Adam of Ebrach, Hildegard reported seeing in a vision 'an extraordinarily beautiful Young Woman wearing shoes which seemed of purest gold whom the whole creation called "Lady". The image spoke to a human person of sapphire blue [possibly Hildegard herself] and said: "Dominion is yours on the day of your power in the radiance of the saints. I have brought you forth from my own womb before the Daystar."' And then Hildegard heard a voice tell her, 'The young woman whom you see is Love. She has her tent in Eternity. For when God wanted to create the world, He bent down with the most tender Love... For it was Love which was the source of this creation in the beginning when God said "Let it be!"' Hildegard asked, 'Why does the whole Creation call this maiden "Lady"?' She received the reply, 'Because it was from Her that all creation proceeded, since Love was the First. She made everything.'

Careful readers of Hildegard and viewers of her illuminations will see deep influences of the ancient goddess religions, of the Roman Aurora, the Egyptian Isis, the old Germanic Horsel, and the Hebrew Hokma, or female Wisdom figure. (Matthew Fox, *Illuminations of Hildegard of Bingen*, pp9-16.)

LIBRA

21 September
[Egyptian]
Ma'at
Goddess who protects Truth with her outstretched wings. She sits on the fulcrum of the scales that balance the deeds of the heart against her one white feather. [Ed.]

[Greek]
Dike
The Greeks call Virgo Dike (Justitia), beccause she is thought to hold the neighbouring Scales. (Eisler, *The Royal Art of Astrology*, p99.)

[Roman]
Astraea
It is fabled that The Starry Goddess, Astraea, returned in the iron age as the impersonation of Justice, whose symbol was the Scales, to praise the equity of Augustus. (Brewer, *Dictionary*.)

23 September
Autumn Equinox
The Greater Eleusinian Mysteries — Day One of Nine Days
[Greek/Roman]
Demeter and Persephone-Kore/Ceres and Proserpine
The Lesser Eleusinian Mysteries were celebrated in February (from the

Figure 72   Libra, Upholder of Justice: Trump VIII of the Egyptian Tarot Pack: Ag Müller.

first day of Aries, where formerly in c.2000 BC it was the first day of Taurus): the Greater in September (from the first day of Libra, where formerly in c.2000 BC it was the first day of Virgo -Ed.)

'I was saying that we ought not to suppose that the ancients appointed the season of the rites irrationally, but rather as far as possible with plausible and true grounds of reason; and indeed a proof of this is that the Goddess Herself chose as Her province the cycle of the Equinox. For the most holy and secret Mysteries of Dea and Kore are celebrated when the sun is in the sign of Libra, and this is quite natural.' (Julian, *Hymn to the Mother of the Gods*, 173A.)

A year after the initiation of the Lesser Mysteries they... were admitted to the Greater. Persons of both sexes and all ages were admitted at this solemnity, and it was looked upon as a heinous crime to neglect this. (Lempriere, *Dictionary*.)

The Athenians were solicitous to secure these advantages to their children, by having them initiated as soon as was allowed. (*Encyclopaedia Britannica*, 1810 edn.)

The Eleusinia were carried from Eleusis to Rome in the age of Hadrian, where they were observed with the same ceremonies as before, though perhaps with more freedom. (Lempriere, *Dictionary*.)

At last the gate became wider, and crowds of people, of all nations, kindreds and languages, provided their character was fair and irreproachable, rushed in by it. (*Encyclopaedia Britannica*, 1810 edn.)

The Mysteries of Eleusis by the latter half of the fourth century AD were thought to hold the entire human race together, 'not only because people continued, no doubt, to come from every corner of the earth to be initiated, as they had in the days of the Emperor Hadrian, but also because the Mysteries touched on something that was common to all men. They were connected not only with Athenian and Greek existence but with human existence in general. And Praetextatus clearly stated just this: *Bios* (Life), he declared would be *abiotos* (unliveable) for the Greeks if the celebration were to cease.' (Zosimus, *Historia Nova* IV, 33.)

Some days before the commencement of the Festival, the public criers invited all the initiated and all pretenders to that honour to attend the festival, with clean hands and a pure heart. (*Encyclopaedia Britannica*, 1810 edn.)

On the first day, called the Day of Assembly, a gathering was held of candidates for initiation... Certain instructions were then given by mystagogues (guides to the Mysteries) as to the various acts and formulas, a knowledge of which was necessary in the course of the initiation. (Butterworth, *Clement of Alexandria*, p383.)

On this day there was a solemn cavalcade of Athenian matrons from Athens to Eleusis, in carriages drawn by oxen. In this procession the ladies used to rally one another in loose terms, in imitation, we suppose, of the Isaic procession described by Herodotus... The most remarkable object in this procession was the Mundus Cereris, contained in a small coffer or basket. This was carried by a select company of Athenian matrons, who, from their office, were styled *Camphorae*. In this coffer were lodged the comb of Ceres, her mirror, a serpentine figure, some wheat and barley... the procession ended at the temple, where this sacred charge was deposited with the greatest solemnity. (*Encyclopaedia Britannica*, 1810 edn.)

[Palestinian]

The Jewish Civil New Year begins on Tishri 1, in September/ October.

24 September

Greater Eleusinian Mysteries — Day Two of Nine Days
[Greek/Roman]

Demeter and Persephone

The second day was called *halade mystai*, (*to the sea ye initiated!*) because they were commanded to purify themselves by bathing in the sea. (Lempriere, *Dictionary.*)

'Washing is the channel through which they are initiated into the sacred rites of Isis or Mithras... at the Eleusinia they are baptized to achieve regeneration and the remission of their sins.' (Tertullian, quoted Larson, *Religion of the Occident*, p183.)

The candidates for initiation bathed themselves in holy water, and put on new clothes, all of linen... From the ceremony of bathing they were denominated *hydrani*, and this was a kind of baptismal ablution. Whether the phrases of 'washing away sin'... 'putting off the old man with his deeds, putting on a robe of righteousness', the words 'mystery', 'perfect', 'perfection', which occur so frequently in the New Testament are borrowed from the Pagan mysteries, or from usage current among the Jews, we leave to our more learned readers to determine. (*Encyclopaedia Britannica*, 1810 edn.)

Among the Greeks and the people of the East, nothing was held more sacred than what were called the *Mysteries*. This circumstance led the Christians, in order to impart dignity to their religion, to say that they also had similar *mysteries*, or certain holy rites, concealed from the vulgar;

and they not only applied the terms used in the pagan mysteries to the Christian institutions, particularly Baptism and the Supper; but they gradually introduced also the rites which were designated by those terms. This practice originated in the Eastern provinces; and thence, after the times of Adrian, who first introduced the Grecian mysteries among the Latins, it spread among the Christians of the West. A large part, therefore, of the Christian observances and institutions, even in the second century, had the aspect of pagan mysteries. (Mosheim, *Ecclesiastical History* I, p173.)

25 September

Greater Eleusinian Mysteries — Day Three of Nine Days

[Greek/Roman]

Demeter and Persephone

On the third day offerings are made, also barley from a field of Eleusis. (Lempriere, *Dictionary*.)

26 September

Greater Eleusinian Mysteries — Day Four of Nine Days

[Greek/Roman]

Demeter/Proserpine

On the fourth day they made a solemn procession, in which the *kalathion*, or holy basket of Ceres, was carried about in a consecrated cart, while on every side the people shouted, 'Hail Ceres!' (*Chaire Demeter!*). After these followed women called *kistophoroi*, who carried baskets in which were sesamum, carded wool, grains of salt, a serpent, pomegranates, reeds, ivy boughs, certain cakes, etc. (Lempriere, *Dictionary*.)

27 September

Greater Eleusinian Mysteries — Day Five of Nine Days

[Greek/Roman]
Demeter and Persephone

In the morning the procession of mystai assembled and left the city by way of the potters' quarter and the Sacred Gate, and marched along the Sacred Road to Eleusis, where it arrived in the evening. (Kerenyi, *Eleusis*, p62.)

The fifth day was called 'the torch day' because in the night following the people ran about with torches in their hands. It was usual to dedicate torches to Ceres, and contend which should offer the biggest in commemoration of the travels of the goddess, and of her lighting a torch in the flames of Mount Etna. (Lempriere, *Dictionary*.)

Figure 73 Persephone holds out in one hand the torch to light the Way, and in the other the pomegranate of immortality. An Etruscan bronze of 560 BC: British Museum.

28 September

Greater Eleusinian Mysteries — Day Six of Nine Days (Holy Night)

[Greek/Roman]

Demeter and Persephone

The sixth day was called 'Iacchos', from Iacchos, who accompanied his mother in search of Persephone with a torch in his hand. From that circumstance his statue had a torch in its hand and was carried in solemn procession from the Kerameikos to Eleusis... In the way nothing was heard but singing and the noise of brazen kettles, as the votaries danced along. The way through which they issued from the city was called *hiera hodos*, 'The Sacred Way', the resting place *hiera syke*, 'sacred fig', from the fig tree which grew in the neighbourhood. They also stopped on a bridge over the Cephisus... After they had passed this bridge they entered Eleusis by a place called *mystike eisodos*, 'The Entrance of the Mysteries'. (Lempriere, *Dictionary*.)

We do not know precisely what sort of sacred objects had been brought from Eleusis to Athens five days before, but only that after crossing the Athenian border, those bearing them had stopped by the sacred fig tree. But the choice of the site probably had to do with these objects. They had been kept for a time in the Eleusinion of Athens, and were carried back to Eleusis in the procession. The priestesses bore them on their heads in baskets. Statues of these basket bearers flanked the inside of the gate leading into the sacred precinct.

We should know still less but for the discovery of a painting, the gift of a certain Ninnion, representing the procession (*myesis*). It shows Iacchos and the goddess Hekate, both bearing torches, leading the initiates — men and women — towards the great Goddesses of Eleusis. In dark clothing and bearing pilgrim's staffs like the simplest of wanderers, the mystai follow in the steps of the grieving goddesses. (White garments were only introduced into the festival in 168 BC. Probably this was due to the influence of the Egyptian mysteries, the cult of Isis, of which such white garments were characteristic.) Already in the classical period the garments worn on the occasion of the *myesis* were held in high esteem. They were dedicated to the goddesses or kept as swaddling clothes for the new generation, although they were the simplest sort of dress, as worn by beggars and wayfarers. Apart from the myrtle boughs in the hair, the mystai are identified as such by two other signs: the women bear vessels filled with *kykeon* [the sacred drink made of a wheaten gruel blended with mint] carefully bound to their heads, and in the hands of the men we recognize the little pitcher which Herakles, Hermes, and the gods of Agrai held in their hands.

It was a kind of procession of spirits, cloaked in a veil of secrecy, which became more and more dense as the mystai approached Eleusis. On the bridge the procession was awaited by mockery and strange games... It was the moment to drink of the *kykeon* which the women had brought along on their heads... A second watercourse was also crossed by a bridge... Here in all probability the mystai had to identify themselves with the words that have come down to us as their password and sign of recognition (*synthema*): they are a summary of everything the initiated had to do before being admitted to the *epopteia* (the Divine Vision). (Kerenyi, *Eleusis*, p62.)

In the form that it has come down to us, reported by Clement of Alexandria, the *synthemon* remains cryptic:

> I have fasted. I have drunk the kykeon. I have reached
> into the big basket and, having worked therein, left
> a residue in the small basket. Then, withdrawing from
> the small basket, I have returned to the large one.

A variant was uttered in the Phrygian Mysteries of Kybele and Attis:

> I have eaten in the tambourine; I have drunk in the
> cymbal; I have carried the vase of compartments; I
> have penetrated beyond the veil (or into the chamber).

[-Ed, from A.Delatte, 'Le Cyceon, breuvage rituel des Mystères d'Eleusis', Paris, 1956]

'Demeter, wandering through Eleusis in search of her daughter, the Maiden... sits down at a well in deep distress. This display of grief is forbidden, up to the present day, to those who are initiated, lest the worshippers should seem to imitate the goddess in her sorrow. Baubo offers Demeter a draught of wine and a meal. She declines to take it, being unwilling to drink on account of her mourning. Baubo is deeply hurt, and thereupon uncovers her secret parts and exhibits them to the goddess. Demeter is pleased at the sight, and now at last receives the draught, delighted with the spectacle. These are the secret mysteries of the Athenians. These are also the subject of Orpheus' poems:

> This said, she drew aside her robes and showed
> Her body all unveiled; child Iacchus was there
> And laughing, plunged his hand below her breasts.
> Then smiled the goddess, in her heart she smiled,
> And drank the draught from out the glancing cup.

'... Consider, too, the contents of the mystic chests... are they not sesame cakes, pyramid and spherical cakes, cakes with many navels, also balls of salt and a serpent? Are they not also pomegranates, fig branches,

Figure 74   Painted on a red-figured skyphos from Athens of c.500 BC, Persephone offers the kykeon, the sacred wheat drink, to Ptolemaeus: British Museum.

fennel stalks, ivy leaves, round cakes and poppies? These are their holy things. In addition, there are the ineffable symbols of Ge Themis, marjoram, a lamp, a sword, and a woman's comb, which is a euphemistic expression used in the mysteries for a woman's secret parts.' (Clement of Alexandria, *Protrept.* XX, 19.)

We now follow the procession through the passage-way. Holding a torch in each hand the Dadouchos, the second priest of the impending great rite, must at nightfall have lighted the way for the procession on its ascending path... Though part of the procession is depicted on the remains of a pedestal... we possess no representation of the whole procession that might have shown us all the priestly dignitaries at its head: the Hierophant, the Dadouchos, the priestesses, and the Hierokerykes, or Mystery Heralds, who preceded the rest. But it is certain that they all took part, and that the Holy Night had already begun when they reached the dancing ground outside the walls of the sacred precinct... On Ninnion's tablet, Demeter received the arriving *mystai* near the *omphalos*. In radiant colour, she is sitting on a rock... Beside her a soft seat is prepared for her daughter, who, painted in dark colours, sits enthroned in the background: the true Queen of the Underworld. (Kerenyi, *Eleusis*, pp75, 79.)

The *mystai* now stream towards the Telesterion (the initiation hall). The building bore a roof with a peak which could be opened to serve as a chimney. On the Holy Night great fire and smoke burst forth from it, breaking the secrecy of the Mysteries. Here took place the *Epopteia*, The Beatific Vision. What was seen has been preserved in the words of Herakles in a papyrus fragment from an oration of Hadrian's time:

> [I have beheld] the fire, whence... [and] I have seen the Kore.

> (Kerenyi, *Eleusis*, p88.)

The Beatific Vision took place in the Anaktoron, a small edifice within the Telesterion. 'Until thou hast reached the Anaktoron, thou hast not been initiated', wrote the orator, Maximos of Tyre. It has been possible to determine precisely the situation and orientation of the throne on which the Hierophant sat, or in front of which he stood, when, like the Bishop of the Christian liturgy, he officiated at the ceremony. The nature of his office is expressed in his title: strictly speaking *hierophantes* means not he who 'shows the holy things', but 'he who makes them appear'. His throne, to the right of the single door of the Anaktoron, was turned towards it. There can be no doubt that what he 'made to appear' came out from there. On the other three sides the throne was screened off: no other impression must distract the Hierophant in his concentration on the awaited epiphany... The smaller edifice with its secrets must have been opened at a word from the Hierophant. A great light burst forth, a fire blazed up; but it is certain that this was not yet the ineffable, holy apparition that was to appear. Many authors speak of this fire... The Queen of the Underworld would be called...

At Eleusis it must have been the Hierophant who intoned the call for Kore. He beat the *echeion*, the instrument with the voice of thunder. The *Epopteia* began; ineffable things were seen. Another papyrus fragment (Milan 20, l.31) gives only a fleeting idea: a figure rose above the ground. According to Plutarch, the initiates underwent a complete transformation: they acted as it was fitting to act in the presence of the Deity. (Kerenyi, *Eleusis*, pp75–94.)

It is by virtue of the nearness of the Goddesses, and finally of their *presence*, that the initiates will have the unforgettable experience of initiation. (Eliade, *Rites and Symbols of Initiation.*)

There is undeniable evidence that the *Epopteia* conferred happiness. Unquestionably *beatitudo*... was engendered at once, *hic et nunc*. But it left room for *elpis*, hope and anticipation... Over the inscription on the votive stele of Eukrates are two eyes... Above is the head of a goddess surrounded by red rays. The rays suggest the light in which the goddess appeared... These testimonies show indirectly that the great vision, the *visio beatifica* of Eleusis, was seen with open, corporeal eyes... Persephone was the object of vision.

'The Athenians when initiating (people) into the Eleusinian Mysteries show to those who have been made Epopts the mighty and wonderful and most perfect mystery for an Epopt there — *a harvested ear of corn* — in silence.' (Hippolytus, *Refutatio*, V8, 39.)

Figure 75   The Goddess and her ear of corn on either face of a coin from Metapontum, fourth century BC: courtesy The Trustees of the British Museum.

The showing of the ear of corn may in fact be a symbolic representation of the display of Baubo to Demeter, regarded by Clement of Alexandria as the secret of the Eleusinian Mysteries. The close association between the grains of certain cereals and the vulva is attested in other traditions, such as the Japanese. The physical similarity to the vulva of barley and wheat grains, that have a longitudinal division with cheeks on either side, is obvious. Thus the 'Vision into the Abyss of the Seed' would be the 'Vision of the Feminine Source of Life'.

Another symbolic action of a similar nature appears also to have been performed: By touching a reproduction of a womb, the initiate evidently gained certainty of being reborn from the womb of the Earth Mother and so becoming her very own child. (Kern, Pauly-Wissowa, *Real-Encyclopaedia* XVI, col.1249; after A.Korte.)

In the Mysteries, the male was enabled, through the experience of the creatively transforming and rebearing power of the Great Mother, to experience himself as her son. (Neumann, *The Great Mother*.)

This assumption would explain the cista mystica as representative of the womb, and that in it the action described in the *synthema* was undertaken... According to Theodoretos, Arnobius and Clement of Alexandria, the Yoni, as the Vulva is named by the Hindus, was the sole object of veneration in the Mysteries of Eleusis. (Demosthenes, *On the Crown*.) (See Figure 18.)

The Epoptai having heard and seen everything requisite and taken upon them vows and engagements... were now declared *perfect men*. They were not only perfect, but *regenerated* men. They were crowned with laurel and dismissed with two barbarous words, *Konx ompax*, of which perhaps the Hierophants themselves did not comprehend the import. They had been introduced by the first Egyptian missionaries, and remained in the Sacra after their significance was lost. (*Encylopaedia Britannica*, 1810 edn.)

29 September

Greater Eleusinian Mysteries — Day Seven of Nine Days
[Greek/Roman]
Demeter and Persephone

On the seventh day were sports, in which the victors were rewarded with a measure of barley, as that grain had been first sown at Eleusis. (Lempriere, *Dictionary*.)

30 September

Greater Eleusinian Mysteries — Day Eight of Nine Days
[Greek/Roman]
Demeter and Persephone

On the eighth day the Lesser Mysteries were repeated, because once Aesculapius, at his return from Epidauros from Athens, was initiated by such a repetition. It became customary, therefore, to celebrate them a second time, that such as had not hitherto been initiated might lawfully be admitted. (Lempriere, *Dictionary*.)

1 October

Greater Eleusinian Mysteries — Day Nine of Nine Days

Figure 76   Seated Parian marble statue of Demeter from the Akropolis at Cnidus, Turkey, 330 BC: British Museum.

[Greek/Roman]
Demeter and Persephone

The last day of the Great Mysteries at Eleusis was devoted to plenty in its liquid form. This was the day of the *plemochoai*, 'the pourings of plenty'. So called, also, were the two unstable circular vases that were set up for this ceremony... The *plemochoai* were poured into a cleft in the earth... one vessel was set up in the east, and the other on the west side, and both overturned. The liquid with which they had been filled is not named. (Kerenyi, *Eleusis*.)

In these celebrated rites, although persons of both sexes and all classes were allowed to take part, and participation in them was even obligatory, very few indeed attained the higher and final initiation. The gradation of the Mysteries is given us by Proclus in the fourth book of his *Theology of Plato*. 'The perfective rite, *teletae*, precedes in order the initiation — *myesis* — and the initiation, *epopteia*, or the final apocalypse (revelation).' Theon of Smyrna, in *Mathematica*, divides the mystic rites into five parts: 'The first of which is the preliminary purification; for neither are the Mysteries communicated to all who are willing to receive them — there are certain persons who are prevented by the voice of the crier — since it is necessary that such as are not expelled from the Mysteries should first be refined by certain purifications which the reception of the sacred rites succeeds. The third part is denominated *epopteia*, or reception. And the fourth, which is the end and design of the revelation, is the 'binding of the head and fixing of the crowns' — whether after this the initiated person becomes an hierophant or sustains some other part of the sacerdotal office. But the fifth, which is produced from all these is *friendship and interior communion with the Goddess*.' And this was the last and most aweful of all the Mysteries. (H.P.Blavatsky, *Isis Unveiled* II, p101.)

'I approached the confines of Death; and, having trodden on the threshold of Proserpina, returned, having been carried through all the elements. In the depths of midnight I saw the sun glittering with a splendid light, together with the infernal and supernal gods, and to these divinities approaching, I paid the tribute of devout adoration.' (Apuleius, *The Golden Ass*, xi.)

6 October
[Norman]
St Faith

St Faith of Aquitaine, 6 October c. 1304.

11 October
[Palestine]
The Virgin Mary

In several places in England, as well as on the Continent, relics of the Blessed Virgin's milk were venerated... Quaresimus tells us that not far from the grotto of the Nativity and the church of the Blessed Virgin, at Bethlehem, there is another subterranean grotto, or rather three

Figure 77   The Goddess/Virgin Mary gives nourishing spiritual milk to her worshippers. In this version Isis suckles the young Ptolemy, who is the youthful Pharoah also shown to the side sucking his finger. An exterior relief on the Ptolemaic Temple of Dendereh, Egypt.

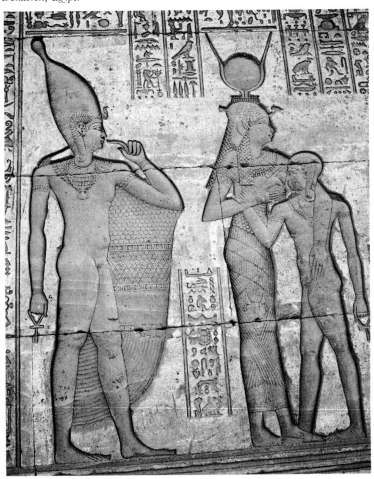

together. An old tradition says that here the Blessed Virgin concealed herself with the Infant Jesus, and that some drops of milk falling from her breast gave miraculous virtue to the rock on which they fell.

This exactly corresponds to the description given by Erasmus in his account of his pilgrimage to Walsingham. He says that the milk was kept in crystal and placed on the high altar... that it was dried up and looked like ground chalk mixed with the white of egg... the prayer that he offered is pious: 'O Virgin Parent, who with they maiden breast hast given milk to thy son Jesus... we beseech thee that... we may also attain to that happy childhood of simplicity which, guileless of malice, fraud, and deceit, earnestly desires the true milk... until it grows into the perfect man.' (Bridgett, *Our Lady's Dowry*, p335.)

13 October
[Portuguese]
Our Lady of Fatima

The last appearance of the Virgin Mary at Fatima took place on 13 October 1917.

The Greater Eleusinian Mystery was, I believe, manifested at Fatima. Here we have people seeing a Golden Disc bringing from the sky the apparition of a woman robed in white. The visions were shown to three children, and occurred on each thirteenth of the month, from May to October; so including the ancient dates of the Mysteries of the Goddesses. At the culmination in October, seventy thousand onlookers saw a sun disc revolve and show spectroscopic change; they called it 'the dancing sun'. (Olivia Robertson, *The Call of Isis*, p125.)

'It is already time that each one of us accomplishes holy deeds of his own initiative and reforms his life according to Our Lady's appeal... She told me that when the other means are exhausted and despised by men, She is giving us the last anchor of salvation, that is the Holy Virgin in person.' (Lucy of Fatima, quoted in Steiger, *Gods of Aquarius*, p67.)

15 October
[Spanish]
St Teresa of Avila

Born October 15 1515 and died October 15 1582.

16 October

[Greek]

Pandrosus

The first priestess of Athena.

SCORPIO

21 October

[Egyptian]

Selket

The Egyptian sky-diagram, first found on a coffin-fragment excavated in Asyut of about 2050 BC shows above the Lion a Scorpion-Goddess, identifiable with the Babylonian goddess Ishhara. (Eisler, *The Royal Art of Astrology*.)

Selket heralded the sunrise through her temples at the autumn equinox about 3700–3500 BC and was the symbol of Isis in the pyramid ceremonials. (Allen, *Star Names*, p361.)

[Mesopotamian]

Ishhara

Scorpio was known to the Babylonians as the female scorpion, the wife of the Archer. (Eisler, *The Royal Art of Astrology*, p102.)

[Greek]

Demeter

The month for sowing, in the season of the Pleiades, the Egyptians call Athyr (sacred to Hathor), the Athenians Pyanepsion and the Beoeotians Damatrios, 'the month sacred to Demeter'.

31 October

The Isia — Day One of Four Days
Samhain Eve — Day One of Three Days

[Egyptian]
Isis

We know that Isis, like Demeter, had two great festivals, one in the spring and another in the autumn. The autumnal celebration consisted of a passion play which continued for four days — although the date varied in different places, it usually began on October 31st and ended on November 3rd. On the first day, actors impersonating Isis, Nephthys, Anubis, Horus, etc., searched for the body of Osiris. (Larson, *Religion of the Occident.*)

'They say, then, that the disappearance of Osiris occurred in the Month of Athyr. As the nights grow longer, the darkness increases, and the potency of the light is abated and subdued. Then among the gloomy rites which the priests perform, they shroud the gilded image of a cow with a black linen vestment, and display her as a sign of mourning for the goddess, inasmuch as they regard both the cow and the earth as the image (eikon) of Isis; and this is continued for four days consecutively.' (Plutarch, *De Iside et Osiride*, 366 D.)

From the account given us by Plutarch, it is clear that the 'Seeking and Finding' of the body of Osiris... was in his day not so much a hidden mystery as a public performance... we may plausibly believe that the ritual of the 'Seeking and Finding' was elaborated in the Ptolemaic age

Figure 78   Isis as the Scorpioness on the lid of a bronze container for a dead scorpion, Ptolemaic Egypt: British Museum.

in conformity with the closer associations between Isis and Demeter. We must remember, however, that it was not conducted in strict secrecy, for it was an undisguised pageant of the resurrection of Osiris performed by Isis, a drama out of doors. (Witt, *Isis in the Graeco-Roman World*, p162.)

'Come to thy house, Come to thy house. O god On, come to thy house, thou who hast no foes. O fair youth, come to thy house, that thou mayest see me. I am thy sister, whom thou lovest; thou shalt not part from me. O fair boy, come to thy house... yet doth my heart yearn after thee and mine eyes desire thee. Come to her who loves thee, who loves thee, Unnefer, blessed one! Come to thy sister, come to thy wife, to thy wife... Come to thy housewife. I am thy sister by the same mother, thou shalt not be far from me. Gods and men have buried their faces towards thee and weep for thee together... I call after thee and weep... yet am I thy sister, whom thou didst love on earth... my brother, my brother.' (A Lament of Isis, quoted Frazer, *Golden Bough* abgd, p366.)

[Mesopotamian]
Bau/Gula

In the old days of Gudea of Lagash the year commenced with the festival of the goddess Bau in the middle of October; in the later Babylon of Hammurabi the feast was transferred to the spring, and the first month of the year began in March. But the older calendar of Babylonia had been already carried to the West... the ancient Canaanite year began in the autumn in what the later calendar reckoned the seventh month... At Lagash it was Bau to whom the festival of the New Year was sacred. (Sayce, *The Religion of Ancient Egypt and Babylon*, p437.)

The festal calendar of Lagash going back to Sumerian times is well-known. There the New Year Festival was celebrated with the marriage of the goddess Bau to the god Ningirsu. (Hooke, *Babylonian and Assyrian Religion*, p53.)

[European]
The Goddess

Samhain, All-Hallows, is the feast of the dead in pagan and Christian times, signalising the close of harvest and the initiation of the winter season, lasting until May. The fairies (*aos sidhe*) were imagined as particularly active at this season, from which the half-year is reckoned. (Dineen, *Dictionary*.)

The feast dates back to the period of time which the Ultonians devoted to the holding of the fair of Samhain in the plain of Murthemne (County Louth) every year: and nothing whatever was done by them during that time but games and races, pleasure and amusement, eating and

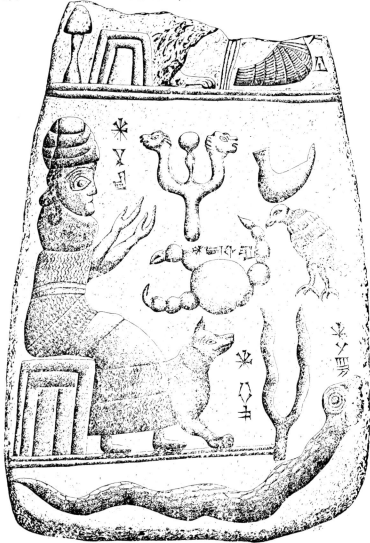

Figure 79   A boundary stone from Mesopotamia shows the Dog Star Goddess of the Autumn Equinox, Bau, surrounded by heavenly symbols.

feasting: and it is from this circumstance that the *Trenae Samna* (three days of Samhain) are still observed throughout Erin. (Joyce, *Social History of Ireland*, II, p438.)

All Celtic feasts begin on their eve... its activities still mark Hallowe'en as one of the great 'spirit nights' of the Celtic peoples. (*The Druids' Calendar.*)

The Fire Festivals are distinctly Female in nature. Samhain is the festival of Hecate, the Old Moon Goddess. (McLean, *Fire Festivals*, p7.)

Red Hanrahan on Samhain Night came to the point where he could walk no longer, so sat down on the heather where he was, in the heart of Slieve Echtge. And after a while he took notice that there was a door close to him, and a light coming from it, and he wondered that being so close to him he had not seen it before. And he rose up and, tired as he was, went in at the door, and although it was night-time outside, it was daylight he found within. And presently he met with an old man that had been gathering summer thyme and yellow flag-flowers, and it seemed as if all the sweet smells of summer were with him.

And with that he brought him into a very big shining house, and every grand thing that Hanrahan had ever heard of, and every colour he had ever seen, was in it. There was a high place at the end of the house, and on it there was sitting in a high chair a woman, the most beautiful the world ever saw, having a blond pale face and flowers about it, but she had the tired look of one that had been long waiting. And there were sitting on the step below her chair four grey old women, and the one of them was holding a great cauldron in her lap; and another a great stone upon her knees, and heavy as it was it seemed light to her; and another of them had a very long spear that was made of pointed wood; and the last of them had a sword that was without a scabbard. Then the first of the old women rose up, holding the cauldron between her two hands, and she said, 'Pleasure'; then the second old woman rose up with the stone in her arms and she said, 'Power'; and the third old woman rose up with a spear in her hand, and she said, 'Courage'; and the last of the old women rose up having the sword in her hands, and she said, 'Knowledge'. And then the four old women went out of the door bringing their four treasures with them. (Yeats, *Mythologies*, p220.)

Tlachtga

Tlachtga also had a feast dedicated to her. The local mother goddesses of Ireland were then the patrons of the great seasonal feasts and assemblies. (Ross, *Pagan Celtic Britain*, p227.)

King Tuathal Teachtmhar in the year 79 of this era built the royal seat of Tlachtga, where the fire Tlachtga was ordained to be kindled. The use of this sacred fire was to summon the priests, augurs and druids of Ireland to repair thither and assemble upon the eve of All Saints. No other fire should be kindled upon that night throughout the kingdom, so that the fire that was to be used in the country was to be derived from this holy fire. (Keating, *A General History of Ireland*, II, p440.)

Hallowe'en was perhaps of old the most important feast, since the Celts would seem to have dated the beginning of the year from it rather than Beltane... In ancient Ireland, a new fire used to be kindled every year on Hallowe'en on the Eve of Samhain, and from this sacred flame all the fires in Ireland were kindled. Such a custom points strongly to Samhain (the first of November) as New Year's Day. (Frazer, *Golden Bough* abgd, p633.)

On All Souls' Eve the living reached out to the souls of the dead and hoped by the pressure of their willing to break down for one night the frontier between the two kingdoms, and enable those on the far side to return. Families sat up and little cakes, known as Soul Cakes, were eaten by everyone. There were still a few children in 1938, going from door to door 'souling' for cakes or money by singing a song. As the clock struck twelve there was silence, for at this hour the souls of the dead would revisit their earthly homes. There were candles burning in every room to guide them... and there was a glass of wine on the table to refresh them. But even though the room became crowded with invisible faces, no-one looked for the wine to diminish by even a hair's breadth during the vigil. (Whistler, *English Festivals*, p198.)

1 November

Isia — Day Two of Four Days
Samhain — Day Two of Three Days

[Egyptian]

Isis

The autumn festival of Isis lasted from three to five days. The fourteen portions of Osiris which had been scattered throughout Egypt by Seth were sought and found by Isis, reconstituted and resurrected. This was the central element in the myth, for if Osiris could regain life and become immortal through the power of Isis, then all her devotees could do the same. (Larson, *Religion of the Occident.*)

Of all the celebrations connected with the worship of Isis the most stirring and most suggestive was the commemoration of the Finding of Osiris. Since the XIIth Dynasty, and probably much earlier, there had been held at Abydos and elsewhere a sacred performance in which the events of Osiris' passion and resurrection were reproduced. The same myth was represented in almost the same manner at Rome at the beginning of each November. (Cumont, *Oriental Religion*, p97.)

'As the winter solstice draws near they lead the [black-veiled golden] cow seven times round the temple of Helios and this perambulation is called the seeking for Osiris.' (Plutarch, *De Iside et Osiride*, 3/2C.)

[Celtic]
Tea
The Assembly of Tara, the ancient religious and political centre of Ireland, was under the patronage of the goddess Tea, and took place on Samhain. There is a tradition in early Irish legends of holding the sacred feast of Samhain on the shores of lakes. In the story of *The Dream of Angus* the feast is held by the side of Loch Bel Dracon — swan-girls with their magic necklets are described, as are the great preparations which went into the making of the feast. (Ross, *Pagan Celtic Britain*, pp23, 227.)

[European]
All Saints
The Church celebrates the presence of All Saints and All Souls following the vigil of All Souls' Eve.

2 November
Isia — Day Three of Four Days
Samhain — Day Three of Three Days
[Egyptian]
Isis
On the third day of the Seeking of Osiris the celebrants 'go down to the sea at night-time; and the keepers of the robes and the priests bring forth the hallowed chest containing a small golden coffer, into which they pour some drinkable water which they have taken up, and a great shout arises from the company for joy that Osiris is found. Then they knead some fertile soil with the water and mix in spices and incense of a very costly sort, and fashion therefrom a crescent-shaped figure which they clothe and adorn.' (Plutarch, *De Iside et Osiride*, 366 F.)

This was a public occasion, marked in the Roman calendar with the name *Hilaria*, because the crowd shouted for joy, 'Osiris has been found!' (Witt, *Isis in the Graeco-Roman World*, p213.)

[European]
All Souls' Day
The feast of All Saints on November 1st was instituted in the ninth century, and the feast of All Souls' Day on November 2nd in 998 AD. (Whistler, *English Festivals*, p198.)

3 November
Isia — Day Four of Four Days (The Hilaria)
Gaelic New Year's Day

[Egyptian]
Isis

Then Isis fanned the cold clay with her wings, breathed her own life into the nostrils of Osiris and with the help of Thoth accomplished the resurrection of Osiris to a second and eternal life. As he lay there reconstituted she fluttered over his erect phallus in the form of a kite and engendered upon herself the golden falcon, Horus, who was to avenge the death of his father. (—Ed)

The fourth day of the festival was called the Hilaria and given over to the most unrestrained rejoicing, since the god, now risen to immortality, would assess all who had become divine by drinking the milk of Isis. And there could be little doubt concerning the future felicity of those who put their trust in her. (Larson, *Religion of the Occident*.)

10 November
[French]
Reason

On November 10th 1793 a festival was held in Notre Dame de Paris in honour of Reason and Liberty, represented by women. Mlle Candeille wore a red Phrygian cap, a white frock, a blue mantle, and tricolour ribbons. Her head was filleted with oak-leaves, and in her hand she carried the pike of Jupiter-Peuple. In the cathedral a sort of 'Temple of Philosophy' was erected on a mound, and in this temple Mlle Candeille was installed. Young girls crowned with oak-leaves were her attendants, and sang hymns in her honour. (Brewer, *Dictionary*.)

With the goddess borne on the shoulders of four citizens, the participants and spectators set off for the convention. Similar ceremonies took place all over the country, where many churches had been converted into temples of Reason. (McIntosh, *Religious History of Modern France*.)

Figure 80 Leonardo da Vinci painted the Virgin Mary as if in an apparition before a grotto of rocks in the early sixteenth century in Italy. This detail shows Her divine face that heals the troubled soul: courtesy The Trustees of the National Gallery, London.

13 November

[Spanish]
Our Lady of Carmel, Garabandal

(Received by Conchita) 'She is dressed in a white robe with a blue mantle and a crown of golden stars. Her hands are slender. Her hair, deep nut-brown, is parted in the centre. Her face is long, with a fine nose. Her mouth is very pretty with lips a bit thin. She looks like a girl of eighteen. She is rather tall. There is no voice like hers. "Have confidence in Us... I am not coming only for you, Conchita, but I am coming for all my children."' (Steiger, *Gods of Aquarius*, pp65, 67.)

SAGITTARIUS

21 November
[Roman]

Artemis/Diana

The Romans assigned the virgin goddess of hunting, Diana, to Sagittarius. (Allen, *Star Names*, p356.)

Samhain

The goddess of the first day of winter. Several Irish authors derive the name Samhain from the Semitic word Shamiyim, or with the Phoenician Samen, or Heaven. (O'Reilly, *Dictionary*.)

The Cailleach

The three months of winter, from Samhain to Brigantia, were under the power and government of the Cailleach, or Old Veiled Woman

Figure 81   In this Babylonian cylinder sealing, a priest propitiates the Sagittarian Goddess standing on her lion, holding bow and arrows: courtesy The Trustees of the British Museum.

Goddess. She was pictured as residing in certain high mountains, and embodies the forces of contraction. (McLean, *Fire Festivals*, p16.)

[Egyptian]
The Goddess as the Days of the Month: The Waxing Moon

In an illustration entitled 'The Divinities of the fourteen days of the Waxing Moon' there is shown a flight of steps rising to the right, and on each of these steps stands a goddess or god holding an Ankh and a Was-sceptre. On the first and lowest step is shown a goddess wearing a disc set between cow's horns, the emblem of Hathor, and later of Isis. (Budge, *Gods of Egypt* II, p321.)

[Palestinian]
The Virgin Mary

Feast of the Presentation of the Virgin Mary in the Temple of Jerusalem.

'And when the child was three years old, Joachim said, "Let us invite the daughters of Israel, and they shall take each a taper or a lamp, and attend on her." And having come to the temple, they placed her on the first step, and she ascended alone all the steps of the altar: and the high priest received her there, kissed her. And being placed before the altar, she danced with her feet, so that all the house of Israel rejoiced with her, and loved her...'. St Evode and St Germanus assert, as an indubitable tradition of the Greek Church, that Mary had the privilege of entering the Holy of Holies... Hence in some paintings of her early life, the ark of the covenant is placed in the background (being one of the symbols of Mary). (Jameson, *Legends of the Madonna*, pp151-5.)

[Babylonian]
Ishtar

In Babylon the Sabbatu of the moon-goddess was at the full moon, and it was then that she was thought to be menstruating. It is *possible* that her colleges of priestesses menstruated in synchrony with each other and in sympathy with the Moon. (Shuttle and Redgrove, *The Wise Wound*, p155.)

The Sabbaths of the Jews were closely related in their origin to the Babylonian Sabbaths, and the Christian weekly day of rest is directly connected with the Jewish sabbath, even though it is observed on a different day of the week. This historical fact all can readily concede, but it is strange to us to think that the prohibitions connected with 'Sabbath observance' are, in their far-off origins, menstrual taboos connected with the belief that the moon is herself a woman having a monthly period. (Harding, *Women's Mysteries*, p63.)

[Egyptian]
Hathor

The goddess Athor, the Venus of the Egyptians... presided over the Western quarter of Thebes... It was into her arms that the sun [sinking] behind the mountain, was poetically supposed to be received, and in this character answered also to Night. (Bartlett, *The Nile Boat*, p162.)

[Arabian]
Al-Uzzah

'The Great One', the Arabian Venus lies behind the Muslim holy day, which is Friday, always considered a lucky day for marriage. The colours of Muslim flags unconsciously honour the female element in displaying the green, or the *vert*, or the woman's colour, or Friday colour, that of the Muslim Sabbath. This green is that of the Venus of Mecca. (Hargrave Jennings, cited Durdin-Robertson, *Goddesses of Chaldea*, p180.)

[Nordic]
Freya

Freya was esteemed the mother of all the gods. She was worshipped as the goddess of love and pleasure, who bestowed on her votaries a variety of delights, particularly happy marriage and easy childbirths. To Freya the sixth day of the week was consecrated, which still bears her name, Friday. (*Encyclopaedia Britannica*, 1810 edn.)

[Palestinian]
Shekinah

Shekinah, the Lady Queen or Matronit 'assumed the form of a divine queen and bride, who joined them every Friday at dusk to bring them joy and happiness on the Sacred Sabbath... According to Raphael Patai 'Sabbath' is the name of the Goddess who is the consort of the Jewish God. Just as in Tantric Hinduism, so Jehovah had his lover, Sabbath or Shekinah... To this day, in every Jewish temple or synagogue she is welcomed in the Friday evening prayers with the words, 'Come, O bride!' although the old greeting is regarded as a mere poetic expression of uncertain significance.

But the significance is clear. Friday night, the Eve of the Sabbath, is the time when man comes together with his wife and the Shekinah fills the house. The Sabbath itself, Saturday, is kept holy and no masculine business venture or work is undertaken, for this is the time that must exist in the Goddess's holy afterglow of loving intercourse between man and woman.

It was important for Torah scholars to perform marital intercourse precisely on Friday night for the reason that the earthly union was symbolic of the heavenly marriage between [Jehovah] and his Bride, Sabbath, [or Sacred Seventh]. (Shuttle and Redgrove, *The Wise Wound*, quoting Ralph Patai, *The Hebrew Goddess* and Scholem, pp231-4, 305.) From Ashera to the Sabbath, manifestations of the Goddess have survived... Every Sabbath evening [every Moon Quarter] contemporary Jews — the heirs of the Hebrew tribes who originally worshipped Ashera, Ashteroth and Astart-Anath — once again pour libations to the Queen of Heaven. (Bat'ya Podos, *Lady Unique 3*, p34.)

The Virgin Mary

It is at least beyond doubt that before the eleventh century Saturday was considered as peculiarly dedicated to the Mother. 'A beautiful custom has grown up in some churches', writes St Peter Damian, 'that on every Saturday in Mary's honour Mass is celebrated, unless some feast or ferial in Lent prevent it.' (Bridgett, *Our Lady's Dowry*, p244.)

Near the close of the tenth century, the custom became prevalent among the Latins of celebrating masses and abstaining from flesh on Saturday, in honour of St Mary. (Mosheim, *Ecclesiastical History*, II, p299.)

[Egyptian]
The Celestial Sow

When at the full, about the 15th of each month, the sow fell upon the moon, tore it out of the face of heaven, and cast it, streaming with blood, into the celestial Nile, where it was gradually extinguished, and lost for three days. Then, having been found, restored to heaven and grown full again, the sow again attacked, and the process renewed.

This Egyptian interpretation demonstrates the close connection to be seen between the lunar monthly circuit and the female menstrual cycle. (Maspero, *Dawn of Civilisation*, p92.)

'Menstruation' means 'moon-change' — in mediaeval times it was taken for granted that the moon's phases are related to the period and that women naturally menstruated in the dark of the moon. Aristotle's books were the standard texts, and the statement is to be found there. (Shuttle and Redgrove, *The Wise Wound*, p155.)

[Mesopotamian]
Ishtar

Ishtar is described as descending the steps of the moon, so many days up and so many down - of these there would be fifteen altogether. At fifteen days of age it was the mother-moon. Hence Ishtar, in Akkad, is designated 'Goddess Fifteen'. These steps are the familiar lunar mansions. (Massey, *Tracts*.)

[Palestinian]
The Virgin Mary

In pictures of the Presentation of the Blessed Virgin Mary as a child at the Temple at Jerusalem the number of steps of the temple is traditionally shown as fifteen. This is also the number of steps of the Moon from which the goddess Ishtar of Babylon is believed to derive her title, 'Goddess Fifteen'. In some Lives of the Virgin Mary the date of her birth is given as the 15th of Hathor. (Author)

The Virgin is called by orthodox Catholic Fathers, The Moon of the Church, Our Moon, Spiritual Moon, The Perfect and Eternal Moon... Innocent III makes the identification still more complete: 'Towards the Moon it is he should look... Let him address himself to Mary.' (Briffault, *The Mothers* III, p184.)

Figure 82   The Moon Goddess, Manat, from Hatra, second century: courtesy the Iraqi Cultural Centre, London.

[Arabian]

Manat/Allaat

Manat was the Arabian Goddess of the Moon, and when combined with the powers of Venus was known as Allaat — *spelt* in exactly the same way as the present Arabic word for God, Allaah. The Goddess is implicitly the foundation of Islam, whether present-day Arabs will confirm or deny it... [-Ed]

[Egyptian]

Goddess as the Days of the Month: The Waning Moon

The Deities of the fourteen days of the waning moon are shown as fourteen squatting women, naked and without head-dresses. They are grouped in two rows of seven, one on top of the other. Each goddess is holding an Ankh. (Budge, *Gods of Egypt*, II, p321.)

[Greek]

Mene/Selene

'And next, sweet-voiced Muses... tell of the long-winged Moon (Mene). From her immortal head a radiance is shown from heaven and embraces earth; and great is the beauty that ariseth from her shining light. The air, unlit before, glows with the light of her golden crown, and her rays beam clear, whensoever bright Selene having bathed her lovely body in the waters of the Ocean and donned her far-gleaming raiment, and yoked her strong-necked, shining team, drives on her long-maned horses at full speed, at eventide in the mid-month; then her great orbit is fulfilled and then her beams shine brightest as she increases... Hail white-armed goddess, bright Selene, mild bright-dressed queen!' (*Homeric Hymns*, XXXII.)

Prosymne

Prosymne is the new moon... Prosymne is Demeter's epithet, the earth mother in her underworld aspect. The Goddess Prosymna was summoned in the name of the new moon when it lingered in the darkness. (Shuttle and Redgrove, *The Wise Wound*, p179.)

Markest thou not? Whenever the Moon with slender horns shines forth in the West, she tells of a new month beginning. (Aratus, *Phaenomena*, p735.)

Hecate

Hecate is generally taken to be the same as the Moon and Proserpine:

hence the epithets Triceps and Triformis given her so often by the Poets, because the Moon sometimes shines full, sometimes disappears quite, and often shows but part of her face. (Davidson on Ovid's *Metamorphoses*, p24.)

The food used to purify the house on the 30th of each month, eggs, onions... were deposited for Hecate at three cross-roads. (Liddle and Scott, *Lexicon*.)

[Roman]

In the Julian Calendar the old divisions of the lunar month were also retained... These were (a) the Kalendae, marking the first appearance of the new moon; (b) the Nonae, marking the first quarter; (c) the Idus, marking the full moon. (Seyffert, *Dictionary*.)

[Mesopotamian]

In Babylon the two most important points of the Moon's course, from the religious point of view, were the full moon (shabattum), and the day of the moon's total disappearance (bubbulum). The latter was marked by fasting, prayers, and other rites. (Hooke, *Babylonian and Assyrian Religion*, p53.)

22nd November
[European]
St Cecilia

A Roman lady of the third century, patroness of music, and of the blind. St Cecilia's musical reputation was well established in the Middle Ages, when the guilds of musicians adopted her as their patron saint. 'The Musical Society' was formed in 1683, partly to keep St Cecilia's Day in worthy manner. Each year on this day, the Society attended a service in London, generally at St Bride's, to enjoy a sermon preached in defence of Cathedral music and an Anthem newly written for the festival. (Whistler, *English Festivals*, p215.)

25 November
[Romano-Egyptian]
St Catherine

St Catherine of Sinai celebrated on this day, a Christian version of Nemesis, Goddess of the Wheel of Fate.

3 December

[Bithynian/Basque]

St Barbara

If the Lady of Amboto, as St Barbara is known in the Basque area, is found in her cave on the day of St Barbara, the following summer will be very good and abundant, but if on that day she is out of her cave, the following summer there will be terrible storms and upsets. (Frank, *Lady Unique* IV, p71.)

8 December

[Egyptian]

Isis

'Immaculate is our Lady Isis', is the legend around an engraving of Serapis and Isis described by King in *The Gnostics and their Remains...* the very terms applied afterwards to the Virgin Mary, who succeeded

Figure 83   An Egyptian sphinx of the Roman period with Nemesis and her wheel on its back: Cairo Museum.

to her form, titles, symbols, rites and ceremonies. Thus her devotees carried into the new priesthood the former badges of their profession, the obligation to celibacy, the tonsure and the surplice, omitting, unfortunately, the frequent ablutions prescribed by the ancient creed. The Black Virgins so highly reverenced in certain French cathedrals... proved, when at last critically examined, to be basalt figures of Isis! (Blavatsky, *Isis Unveiled* II, p95.)

[Greek]

Not only was the Platonic philosophy selected by the Christians as a basis for the trinity... did they not have a ready model for the 'miraculous conception' in the legend about Periktione, Plato's mother? In her case it was also maintained by popular tradition that she had immaculately conceived him, and that the God Apollo was his father. Even the annunciation by an angel to Joseph 'in a dream', the Christians copied from the message of Apollo to Arison, Periktione's husband, that the child to be born from her was the offspring of that God. (Blavatsky, *Isis Unveiled* II, p325.)

[Persian]

Anahita

The Aban Yasht is a Persian Scripture devoted to the Great Goddess of the Waters, Ardvi Sura Anahita (the High, the Powerful, the Undefiled), the Heavenly Spring from which all waters on the earth flow down; her fountains are on the top of the mythical mountain, the Hukairya, in the starry region.

'Oh Ardvi Sura Anahita! With the Haoma and food, with the baresma, with the wisdom of the tongue, with the holy spells, with words, with deeds, with libations and with truly spoken prayers, offer up an oblation, O Spitama Zarathustra.

'She is strong, bright, tall and beautiful of form, who sends down by day and by night a flow of motherly waters as large as the whole of the waters that run along the earth... For her, brightness and glory.

'Come, O Ardvi Sura Anahita, come from those stars down to the earth... that the great lords may worship thee, the masters of the countries.

'She stands, the good Ardvi Sura Anahita, wearing a golden mantle, waiting for a man who shall offer her libations and prayers, and thinking thus in her heart: "Who will praise me?" Ever holding the baresma in her hand according to the rules, she wears golden earrings on her pierced ears, and a golden necklace around her beautiful neck, she, the nobly born Ardvi Sura Anahita; and she girds up her waist tightly, so that her breast may be well-shaped, that they may be tightly pressed. Upon her head she binds a golden crown, with a hundred stars, with light rays... with fillets streaming down.

'I bless the offering and prayer, and the strength and vigour of the Holy Water-Source, Anahita.' (Extracts from Darmesteter, *The Zend Avesta* V.)

[Palestinian]
The Virgin Mary

Feast of the Immaculate Conception of the Blessed Virgin Mary.

In the second half of the sixth century the Byzantines reached the point of decreeing holy days for Mary alone. Her self-conception in her mother St Anne was observed. (Ashe, *The Virgin*, p200.)

It is certain that a feast in honour of Mary's Conception was celebrated in the Eastern Church long before the time of St Anselm... there is no doubt that the propagation of the feast throughout Europe took place especially from the eleventh century, and that the origin of the movement was in England. Nor can there be any question that it was generally attributed to St Anselm. (Bridgett, *Our Lady's Dowry*, p231.)

In the Immaculate Conception the Virgin shares both verbally and visually the attributes of the Goddesses. The dogma itself is suggestive of the Egyptian belief that the primordial goddesses 'proceeded from themselves'. As Maspero (*Dawn of Civilization*, p144) states: 'the epithets applied to them... represent them as having independent creative power by virtue of their own unaided force and energy'. (Jameson, *Legends of the Madonna*.)

There is a particularly close correspondence between the Virgin Mary and the ancient Goddess, Neith/Isis of Sais (Athena in Greece), described as 'the prototype of parthenogenesis'. Thus the Marquis of Mirville states, 'We Catholics understand also how it is that the famous inscription at Sais should have stated that "none ever lifted my veil", considering that this sentence, literally translated, is the summary of what is sung in the Church on the day of the Immaculate Conception.'
  In the iconography of the Immaculate Conception there is to be seen from the Virgin's emblems an intimate association with the Goddesses. For instance, the stars around her appear on the Egyptian Sky-goddess Nut, the rose and mirror are attributes of Isis, the olive of Athena, the crescent moon of Artemis. (Blavatsky, *The Secret Doctrine*, II, p108.)

The Great She-Bear Shamaness

She envisages her birth into the human dimension from the celestial plane as an alteration in the cosmos... She, the Grandmother of the race... In this second coming where woman is born of woman and to woman through her own election, she awakens to a world recreated in her own image. (Orenstein, *Lady Unique*, V, 50.)

9 December
[Mexican]
The Virgin of Guadalupe
Many archaeologists regard Her as an old Aztec sky-goddess, in slight disguise. (Wilson, *The Cosmic Trigger*.)

The Virgin of Guadalupe became the patron saint of all Mexico in 1737, the Queen of Mexico in 1895, and Empress of the Americas in 1945. (Turner, *Lady Unique*, I, 47.)

10 December
[French]
Liberty
On December 10th 1793, Mlle Maillard, an actress, was selected to personify the Goddess of Liberty. Being brought to Notre Dame she was seated on the altar, and lighted a large candle to signify that Liberty was the Light of the World. (Brewer, *Dictionary*.)

18 December
The Saturnalia — Day One of Seven Days
[Roman]
Ops
The Goddess of Plenty, old Italian goddess of abundance and wife of Saturn with whom she shared the temple on the Capitol and the festival of the Saturnalia. Celebrations consisted of offerings in the open air in front of the temple and also an outdoor banquet. Schools had holidays, law-courts were closed, all work was stopped, war was deferred, and no punishment of criminals took place for seven days. During this time there were all kinds of fantastic amusements. The festival was symbolic of a return to the Golden Age. People gave presents to one another, in particular wax tapers and dolls. They also entertained one another and amused themselves with social games. Every freedom was given to slaves, and they were first entertained at the banquet and served by their masters, in remembrance that under the rule of Saturn there had been no differences in social rank. (There is a similar army custom today whereby the officers wait on the men.) The priests made their

offerings with heads uncovered, a custom which was never observed at other festivals. It was a priestess who conducted the rites of the Saturnalia at Rome. (Seyffert and Lempriere, *Dictionaries*/Borlase, *Dolmens* III, pp9, 828.)

19 December

The Saturnalia — Day Two of Seven Days

[Roman]

Ops

The Opalia was specifically celebrated on the second day of the Saturnalia. Several of the ceremonies of the Saturnalia season as a whole are continued at the present time during the days leading up to Christmas. The great feast of Saturn and Ops was held in December, when the people decorated the temples with such green things as they could find. Holly used to be employed by the early Christians at Rome to decorate churches and dwellings at Christmas: it had previously been used in the great festival of the Saturnalia, which occurred at the same season of the year. The pagan Romans used to send their friends holly-sprigs with wishes for their health and well-being.

20 December

The Saturnalia — Day Three of Seven Days

Ammit/Al-Mawt

Ammit... originally was the ancestral spirit of the matriarchal culture in which the Feminine takes back what has been born of it... The underworld, the earth womb, as the perilous land of the dead through which the deceased must pass... is one of the archetypal symbols of the Mother. It is experienced in the archetypal nocturnal sea voyage of the sun. (Neumann, *The Great Mother*, p156.)

CAPRICORN

21 December

The Saturnalia — Day Four of Seven Days

The Womb of Isis

The adoration of the Mendesian Goat rehearsed the Sun-God's resurrection in the House of the Goat (Capricorn) — Hr Bnt — The Womb of the Lady. (Grant, *The Magical Revival*, p76.)

[Greek]

Amalthea

Amalthea was the nymph who fed Jupiter with goat's milk, one of whose horns broke off and was placed amongst the stars as Cornu Amaltheae, or Cornu Copiae, from which nectar and ambrosia were said to flow. (White, *Dictionary*.)

This divinity is usually assigned to the stars of Auriga, whose principal star is Capella, the little goat. All this, doubtless, was from oriental legends which made Capricorn the nurse of the youthful sun-god that long anticipated the story of the infant Jupiter and Amalthea. (Allen, *Star Names*, p135.)

Vesta

Capricorn was regarded as under the care of the goddess Vesta, and hence Vestae Sidus. (Allen, *Star Names*, p136.)

[Greek]

Nyx and Hemera

Night and Day: There stands the awful home of murky Night wrapped in dark clouds. In front Night and Day draw near and greet one another as they pass the great threshold of bronze: and while the one is about

Figure 84   Design on a bronze disc pinhead from Luristan c.1000 BC, showing the Capricornian Goddess giving birth to the divine child of the new year.

to go down into the house, the other comes out at the door. And the house never holds them both within; but always one is without the house passing over the earth, while the other stays at home and waits until the time for her journeying comes; and the one holds all-seeing light for them on earth, but the other holds in her arms Sleep, the brother of Death, even fatal Night, wrapped in vaporous cloud. (Hesiod, *Theogony*, p124.)

22 December

The Saturnalia — Day Five of Seven Days
[Greek]

Kore/Persephone

The birth of the Divine Child, whether he bears the name of Horus,

Osiris, Helios, Dionysos or Aeon, was celebrated in the Koreion in Alexandria, the temple dedicated to Kore, on the day of the winter solstice.
(Neumann, *The Great Mother*, p312.)

[Celtic]

Rhiannon

Pryderi, son of Rhiannon, the virgin mother, is always born on the
winter solstice. (Graves, *The White Goddess*, p95.)

23 December

The Saturnalia — Day Six of Seven Days

Larunda

An extremely obscure Roman goddess said to be Sabine, and generally
supposed to be chthonian. She was honoured on this day at an altar
in the Velabrium. (*OCD*)

24 December

The Saturnalia — Day Seven of Seven Days
Christmas Eve

[European]

The Mothers

Modraniht, or 'Night of the Mothers', was so called as the day preceding
'Child's Day' or 'Yule Day' long before the Anglo-Saxons came into
contact with Christianity, thus proving its real character. (Hislop, *The
Two Babylons*.)

Inscriptions are known from Roman times in Germany, Holland and
Britain in honour of groups of female beings known generally as 'The
Mothers'. Female deities of this kind seem to have been worshipped
by both the Celts and the Germans, and they were evidently associated
with fertility and with the protection of hearth and home. (Davidson,
Gods and Myths of Northern Europe, p112.)

25 December
Christmas Day
Yule Eve

[Egyptian]

Isis

The goddess Isis, the Virgo Caelestis, was believed to give birth to the Sun on the 25th of December. (Eisler, *The Royal Art of Astrology*.)

[Mesopotamian]

Astarte

Long before the Christian era a festival was celebrated in honour of the birth of the son of the Babylonian Queen of Heaven. The same festival was adopted by the Roman Church. (Hislop, *The Two Babylons*, p93.)

[Persian]

Atargatis

Mother of Mithra, whose nativity also fell on this day.

[Greek]

Myrrha

The mother of Adonis was mystically said to have been changed into a tree, and when in that state to have brought forth her divine son. And this entirely accounts for the putting of the Yule Log into the fire on Christmas Eve. As Zero-Ashta (Seed of Woman, which name also signifies Ignigena — Born of Fire) he has to enter the fire on 'Mother night' that he may be born the next day out of it. (Hislop, *The Two Babylons*, p97.)

The Girl of the Yule Log

Sometimes the log would be dragged in with a girl enthroned on it, and then there would be glasses raised to Her health. The log will be chosen and cut beforehand: ash that burns green and was therefore sacred to the Sun... Ash that was believed in Scandinavia to be the wood of the world-tree, Yggdrasil, with its roots knotted in Hell and its boughs supporting Heaven. Sometimes it would be sprinkled with corn. (Whistler, *English Festivals*, pp58-9.)

Figure 85   Countless Egyptian sculptures from all periods portray Mother Isis with the Divine Child in her lap: British Museum.

Figure 86   On this Roman coin from Myra the Goddess and the Tree are one: courtesy The Trustees of the British Museum.

The Star Fairy

The Christmas Tree, with its bright baubles and the star on top is a miniature version of the World Tree of our pagan ancestors, with its roots deep in the earth, the sun, moon and stars hung on its spreading branches, and the Pole Star at its topmost point. Sometimes the Star is replaced by a Goddess, ruling over the World. (Valiente, *ABC of Witchcraft*, p323.)

We might see in the Christmas Tree the custom of the Saturnalia introduced by the Roman legions, the pine tree hung with little masks of Bacchus. (Whistler, *English Festivals*, pp58-9.)

The cedar in its bravery is the symbol which the Goddess (i.e. Ishtar) uses repeatedly to express her own attractiveness as she prepares to meet her risen husband. The sacred pole as the symbol of Ishtar, or Astarte, or any other form of the Mother Goddess, is everywhere to be found in the ancient near East. (Hooke, *Babylonian and Assyrian Religion*, p33.)

[Irish]

Nullog

Nullog in Ancient Irish was short for *nul bullog*, meaning 'New Belly'. It was celebrated as Nullog Day to stand for 'being born anew'. Thus for this end it was that they excavated those apertures in the bodies of rocks... or *yonis*, in order that, by passing themselves through them, they might represent the condition of one issuing, through the womb, to a new scope of life.

Another method of symbolization confined solely to the initiated was that which characterized the construction of their subterranean temples. Here the sublimity of their worship breaks out in all the grandeur of majesty and awe. The narrowness of the entrance is never larger than the girth of the ordinary human body... the temple at New Grange is exactly so constructed. After squeezing yourself with much labour through a long emblematic gallery, you arrive at a circular room. (O'Brien, *Round Towers*, p350.)

[European]

The Virgin Mary

At the end of the third or beginning of the fourth century the Western Church adopted this day as the true date of the birth of the Christos, and in time its decision was accepted also by the Eastern Church. (Frazer, *Golden Bough* abgd, p358.)

26 December

Yule — Day One of Twelve Days
[Ancient Gothic]

Yule

A heathen feast lasting twelve days — ultimate origin obscure. (*Oxford English Dictionary*.)

Yule is related to Saxon and Norse words for 'Light', or 'Sun'. It refers to the Festival of the Rebirth of the Light celebrated from this day for twelve days. (Brewer, *Dictionary*.)

According to Bede and other authorities of olden time, the word *Yule* is derived from an old Norse world *Iul*, meaning 'Wheel'. In the old Clog Almanacs, the symbol of a wheel was used to mark Yuletide. The idea behind this is that the year turns like a wheel, the Great Wheel of the Zodiac, the Wheel of Life, of which the spokes are the old ritual occasions, the equinoxes and solstices, and the four 'cross-quarter days' of Candlemas, May Eve, Lammas and Hallowe'en. The winter solstice, the rebirth of the sun, is a particularly important turning point. (Valiente, *ABC of Witchcraft*, p359.) (See Figure 2.)

We are told the ancient Egyptians at the Winter Solstice used a palm branch containing twelve leaves or shoots to symbolize the 'completion of the year'. (Brewer, *Dictionary*.)

Figure 87   Shu, the Atmosphere, separates the Sky Goddess from union with her husband, Geb the Earth: a commonly repeated drawing on Egyptian papyri.

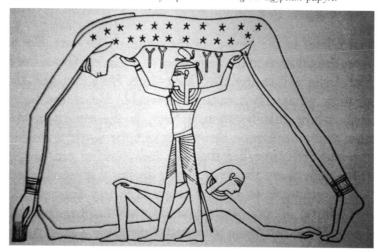

27 December

Yule — Day Two of Twelve Days
lst Intercalary Day

Nut

They intercalated after the twelfth month of each year and before the first day of the ensuing year five epagomenal days... to permit Nut to give birth to all her children. (Maspero, *Dawn of Civilisation*, p208.)

28 December

Yule — Day Three of Twelve Days
2nd Intercalary Day

[Greek]

The Horae

Hora originally meant any limited time or period, especially as fixed by natural laws and revolutions, whether seasons, or times of day such as morning, noon and night. In the definite sense of *an hour*, or the revolution of half a sign of the zodiac during the day, it was probably so used first by Hipparchos c.140 BC. The Horae were sometimes personified as Eunomia, Dike and Eirene, who presided chiefly over all changes of time and watched over the works of men. (Liddell and Scott, *Lexicon*.)

This word Hours, therefore, call'd by the Greeks Horai, signified both the Seasons of the Year and the Hours of the Day... Perhaps these Hours of the Day answer to the Hours of the Year, so that the third Hour denotes the Spring, the sixth, the Summer, the ninth the Autumn, and the Evening, Winter. (Montfaucon, *Ant.Suppl.*, 28.)

The Horae were goddesses of order in nature. They were represented as delicate, joyous, lightly moving beings adorned with flowers and fruits. (Seyffert, *Dictionary*.)

29 December

Yule — Day Four of Twelve Days
3rd Intercalary Day

[Egyptian]

The Hours

The Egyptians were the first to divide the day into 24 hours; there were twelve hours of the day and twelve to the night. Each was allocated a goddess standing in a boat, led by Isis, the Great Enchantress, uttering the words which made the boat proceed on its way through the perils of Time. ...The 'Lady of the Boat' changed every hour, for she represented the local goddess of one hour who was supposed to be the appointed guide ... knowing the way through her own district, she was able to instruct the captain of the boat how and where to sail over difficult reaches of the river. (Gardiner, *Egyptian Grammar*, p206, and Budge, *Gods of the Egyptians* I, pp205, 232.)

Hathor/Nut

As Sky-Goddess Hathor gives birth to the sun Ra, in the form of the Scarab beetle, and in this respect resembles Nut. (Author)

30 December

Yule — Day Five of Twelve Days
4th Intercalary Day

[Egyptian]

Isis

The Egyptian year consisted of twelve months of 30 days each making only 360 days: thus five epagomenal days, sometimes called 'the little month', or 'the thirteenth month', were added to make the year a complete 365. Isis, Goddess of The Throne, governed the fourth intercalary day, which was celebrated as her birthday.

31 December

Yule — Day Six of Twelve Days
5th Intercalary Day
New Year's Eve (Modern Times)

[Egyptian]

Nephthys

The fifth epagomenal day was celebrated as the birthday of Nephthys,

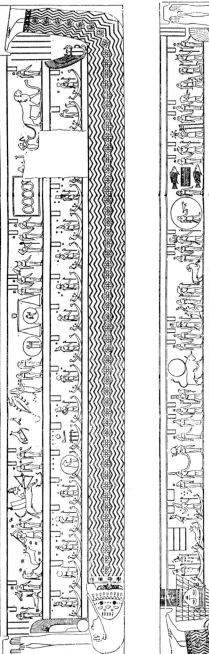
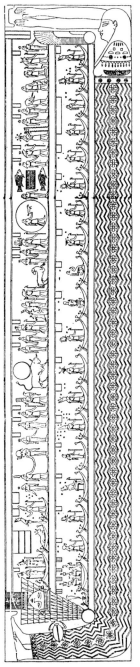

Figure 88 In the rectangular zodiac from the Ptolemaic Temple of Denderah, Nut is represented twice as the sky on the ceiling to the left and right of the hypostyle hall, each torso holding six of the twelve signs of the zodiac. Hathor is indicated at the starting point of the year as the cow-eared goddess witnessing the birth of the sun from the loins of Nut. Near her head the stellar starting point of the year is indicated by Isis leading the 36 decans as the star Sothis — a cow seated in a boat — while Osiris as Orion runs before her.

Figure 89   On an Egyptian Ptolemaic bronze situla, Isis and Nephthys worship Osiris as the Djed Column of the segmented Year: British Museum.

Figure 90   Sekhmet, Goddess of Time, with the Solar disc on her head: Berlin Museum.

Goddess of The House, who was given the name, Teleute, or Finality — the Greek equivalent being Nike. (Plutarch, *De Iside et Osiride*.)

Sekhmet

Goddess of Time: 'Mistress of the Double White Palace: whatsoever thou seest on this day will be fortunate.' (*Sallier Papyrus* iv, cited Maspero, *Dawn of Civilisation*, p211.)

[Greek/Roman]

Hestia/Vesta

Hestia is the Genia of the home-fire, and it is traditional on this day to bless the house by making the Pentacle in the four corners of each room. Ivy is hung on the outer doors to protect the house against evil through the coming year. Hestia is also the Genia of the true home-fire that burns deep within each soul. (*The Coming Age*, p3.)

[Graeco-Egyptian]

To show the connection between country and country, and the inveterate endurance of old customs, it is worthy of remark that Jerome observes that 'It was the custom so late as his time (348-420 AD) in all cities, especially in Egypt and Alexandria, to set tables, and furnish them with luxurious articles of food, and with goblets containing a mixture of new wine, on the last day of the month and year, and that people drew omens from them in respect of the fruitfulness of the year.' The Egyptian year began at a different time from ours, but this is as near as possible the way in which Hogmanay is still observed on the last day of the last month of the year in Scotland. Everybody in the South of Scotland is personally cognisant of the fact that, on Hogmanay, or the evening before New Year's Day, among those who observe old customs, a table is spread, and while buns and other dainties are provided by those who can afford them, oat cakes and cheese are brought forth among those who never see oat cakes but on this occasion, and that strong drink forms an essential article of the provision. (Hislop, *The Two Babylons*, p 95.)

[Scottish]

Hogmanay

New Year's Night preceding the Hagmena, or Holy Month.

[Irish]

Divination of the future was common on New Year's Eve... indeed, almost anything which happened on New Year's Eve and Day might be ominous of the future, and the nearer to the midnight hour when the year actually began, the more significant. (Danaher, *The Year in Ireland*, p259.)

Return to the Beginning

Venus and The Moon

The disposer of all hidden times knows in what revolutions kindly Venus hastens on her way, or how long are the tasks that yet await Phoebe before that which they call The Great Year reaches its close, and the wandering stars come back again in their ancient courses as they stood at the beginning of the ordered universe. (Ausonius, *Eclogues*, v.10.)

Cailleach Bheara

The Age of the Yew Tree corresponds to the infancy of humanity. In this primordial era, life is lived close to the earth and shows little change.

The Age of the Eagle corresonds to the adolescence of humanity. This era, characterized by scientific, political and social aspiration, and also by technical achievement, is one of rapid change.

Figure 91   Time as the Devouring Goddess and bringer of Death is expressed in the Greek Pantheon as the Gorgon. This terra cotta version was an attachment to a Campanian coffin c.480 BC: British Museum.

The Age of Cailleach Bheara corresponds to the maturity of humanity. This is an era of reawakened psychic and artistic sensitivity, of renewed magical powers and of growing religious knowledge. It is, therefore, an age dominated increasingly by the Goddess. (Borlase, *Dolmens* III, p839.)

Figure 92   Isis in her knotted red girdle protects Seti I, a drawing by Ann Calverley of a nineteenth dynasty wall painting in the Chapel of Isis in the Temple of Seti I at Abydos, Egypt: courtesy the Committee of the Egypt Exploration Society, London.

Figure 93   A wooden carving of the She-Serpent, Meret-Seger (She Who Loves Silence),
protectress of The Valley of the Kings, where Time and Death merge in an Eternity
of Millions of Years: British Museum.

The Knot of Isis

At the ends of the universe is a blood-red cord that ties life to death, man to woman, will to destiny. Let the knot of that red sash, which cradles the hips of the Goddess, bind in me the ends of life and dream. I'm an old man with more than my share of hopes and misgivings. Let my thoughts lie together in peace. At my death let the bubbles of blood on my lips taste as sweet as berries. Give me not words of consolation. Give me magic, the fire of one beyond the borders of enchantment. Give me the spell of living well.

Do I lie on the floor of my house or within the temple? Is the hand that soothes me that of wife or priestess? I rise and walk. The sky arcs ever around; the world spreads itself beneath my feet. We are bound mind to Mind, heart to Heart — no difference rises between the shadow of my footsteps and the will of the Divinity. I walk in harmony, heaven in one hand, earth in the other. I am the Knot where two worlds meet. Red magic courses through me like the Blood of Isis, magic of magic, spirit of spirit. I am proof of the power of gods. I am water and dust walking. (Ellis, *Awakening Osiris*, a translation of *The Egyptian Book of the Dead*, Incantation no.55.)

Neheb-Kau
Was worshipped at Hehen-su in the form of a huge serpent with two heads at one end of her body, and one at the other: she was one of the Forty-Two Assessors in the Hall of Judgement of the Goddess Ma'at (Truth). (Budge, *Gods of the Egyptians* II, p62.)

The She-Serpent
I am justified. For I chose wisdom and the knowledge of good and evil. And now there is no evil, and wisdom and good are one. (Shaw, *Back to Methuselah*, p146.)

Ammit
The fire from Ammit corresponds to the serpent fire of the Goddess Kundalini. (Durdin-Robertson, *Goddesses of Chaldaea*, p328.)

Bibliography

For reasons of brevity, the bare titles of books have been given, usually with the date of the most recent edition available at the time of compilation, and with some insertions by the editor/picture researcher of current books on goddesses. As library facilities nowadays are accessible to all, title and author have been deemed sufficient to lead the reader to the edition most suitable for her or his particular needs.

Adler, Margot, *Drawing Down the Moon*, New York, 1979.

Alexander, William, *The History of Women* (2 vols), London, 1779.

Allen, Richard, *Star Names: Their Lore and Meaning*, New York, 1963.

Anderson, George, *A Critical Introduction to The Old Testament*.

Anderson, Robert, *The Story of Extinct Civilizations of the East*, London, c.1903.

The Apocrypha, 1970.

The Apocryphal New Testament, 1966.

Apollodoros, trs. Sir James Frazer, *The Library* (2 vols), Loeb, 1976.

Apuleius, Lucius, trs.Robert Graves, *The Golden Ass*, Harmondsworth, 1950.

Aratus, *Phaenomena*, Loeb, 1977.

Aristophanes, *Thesmophoriazusae*.

Ashe, Geoffrey, *The Virgin*, London, 1976.

The Atlantean (Journal), formerly at 42 St George's Street, Cheltenham, now at Runnings Park, Croft Bank, West Malvern, Worcs.

Augustine of Hippo, *De Civitate Dei*, Harmondsworth, 1972.

Austen, R., *Sufis of Andalusia*, London, 1970.

Ausonius, Decimus, *Writings*, Loeb, 1967-8.

Baigent, M. et al., *The Holy Blood and The Holy Grail*, London, 1980.

Baring-Gould, S., *Curious Myths of the Middle Ages*, London, 1869.

Bartlett, W.H. *The Nile Boat*, London, 1861.

Baseley, G. *A Countryman's Compendium*, Newton Abbot, 1977.

Begg, Ean, *The Cult of the Black Virgin*, London, 1986.

Berger, P., *The Goddess Obscured*, London, 1985.

Bernal, M., *Black Athena* I, London, 1987.

The Bible (Authorized Version), 1611.

Blavatsky, H. *Isis Unveiled* (2 vols), London, repr. 1923.

_____ *The Secret Doctrine*, Adyar, 1888.

Boland, M., *Manuscript on Indian Festivals*, 1974.

The Book of Common Prayer, (Church of England).

The Book of Common Prayer, (Church of Ireland).

Borlase, William, *The Dolmens of Ireland* (3 vols), London, 1897.

Brewer, E., *Brewer's Dictionary of Phrase and Fable*, London, 1894.

Brewer, J.N., *The Beauties of Ireland*, London, 1826.

Bridgett, T., *Our Lady's Dowry*, London, 1875.

Briffault, R., *The Mothers* (abridged edn), London, 1959.

British and Foreign Bible Society, *Old Testament* (Hebrew Text), London.

Brown, F. et al., *A Hebrew and English Lexicon of the New Testament*, Oxford, 1907.

Budge, W., *The Gods of the Egyptians*, London, 1904.

_____ *The Egyptian Book of the Dead*, London, 1909.

Burland, C., *North American Indian Mythology*, London, 1968.

Butterworth (ed.), *Clement of Alexandria*.

Caldecott, Moyra, *Women in Celtic Myth*, 1988.

_____ *Daughter of Amun*, (The story of Queen Hatshepsut), London, 1989.

Callimachus of Cyrene, *Hymns and Epigrams*, Loeb, 1967.

_____ *Aetia*, Loeb, 1975.

Carlisle, N., *A Topographical Dictionary of Ireland*, London, 1810.

Carter, Charles, *The Principles of Astrology*, London, 1925.

Chabas, F. (trs.), *Sallier Papyrus IV*, Paris, 1870.

Ciaceri, E., *Culti e miti nella storia dell'antica Sicilia*, Catania, 1911.

Cicero, *De Natura Deorum*, Loeb, 1972.

_____ *De Divinatione*, Loeb, 1971.

Clement of Alexandria, *Le Protreptique*, Paris, 1949.

Columella, Lucius, *De Re Rustica*, Loeb, 1977.

The Coming Age (Journal), Lux Madriana, formerly 40 St John Street, Oxford.

County Kildare Archaeological Journal.

Crow, W., *The Arcana of Symbolism*, London, 1970.

Cumont, F., *The Oriental Religions in Roman Paganism*, New York, 1956.

Danaher, Kevin, *The Year in Ireland*, Cork, 1972.

Daraul, A., *Secret Societies*, London, 1965.

Davidson, H., *Gods and Myths of Northern Europe*, Harmondsworth, 1969.

Defresnoye, L., *Chronological Tables of Universal History*, London, 1762.

Demosthenes, *On the Crown.*

Denning, M. et al., *The Magical Philosophy*, St Paul, Minnesota, 1974.

Desroches-Noblecourt, C., *Tutankhamun*, London, 1963.

Dineen, P., *An Irish-English Dictionary*, Dublin, 1975.

Ditchfield, *Old English Customs.*

The Druids Calendar, New York, 1979.

Duchesne-Guillemin, J., *La Religion de l'Iran ancien*, Paris, 1962.

Durdin-Robertson, L., *The Cult of the Goddess*, Clonegal, 1975.

_____ *The Goddesses of Chaldaea, Syria and Egypt*, Clonegal, 1975.

_____ *The Goddesses of India, Tibet, China and Japan*, Clonegal, 1975.

_____ *Initiation and the Mysteries*, Clonegal, 1976.

Eisler, Rianne, *The Chalice and the Blade*, San Francisco, 1987.

Eisler, Robert, *The Royal Art of Astrology*, London, 1946.

Eliade, M., *Rites and Symbols of Initiation*, New York, 1958.

Ellis, Normandi, *Awaking Osiris* (a highly recommended recent translation of *The Egyptian Book of the Dead*), London, 1988.

Encyclopaedia Britannica, 4th edn, 1810.

Evans-Wentz, W., *Fairy-Faith.*

_____ *The Tibetan Book of the Dead.*

Fagan, Cyril, *Zodiacs Old and New*, London, 1951.

Farrar, Janet & Stewart, *Eight Sabbats for Witches, and Rites for Birth, Marriage and Death*, London, 1981.

_____ *The Witches' Goddess*, London, 1987.

Farrar, Stewart, *What Witches Do*, London, 1971.

Fox, M., *The Illuminations of Hildegard of Bingen* Santa Fe, 1985.

Frazer, Sir James, *The Golden Bough* (abridged version), London, 1932.

Gardiner, Sir A., *Egyptian Grammar*, Oxford, 1927.

Gimbutas, Marija, *The Goddesses and Gods of Old Europe* (updated), London, 1989.

Goethe, J., *Faust*, Engl. trs. London, 1980.

Grant, K., *The Magical Revival*, 1972.

Graves, Robert, *The White Goddess*, London, 1967.

Green, Marian, *A Harvest of Festivals*, London, 1980.

Gregory, Lady, *Visions and Beliefs in the West of Ireland*, Gerrard's Cross, 1976.

Hanmer, M., *The Chronical of Ireland*, Dublin, 1809.

Harding, Esther, *Women's Mysteries: Ancient and Modern*, London, 1971.

Harrison, Jane, *Themis, A Story of the Social Origins of Greek Religion*, London, 1911.

_____ *Ancient Art and Ritual*, London, 1913.

Hartmann, F., *In the Pronaos of the Temple of Wisdom*, Chicago, 1890.

Heraclitus, *Allegories d'Homere*, Paris, 1962.

Hermes Trismegistus, *The Divine Pymander*, New York, 1972.

Herodotos, *The Histories*, London, 1970.

Hesiod, *Homeric Hymns*, Loeb, 1970.

Hislop, Alexander, *The Two Babylons*, London, 1965.

Homer, *The Iliad*, Harmondsworth, 1950.

_____ *The Odyssey*, London, 1913.

Hooke, S.H., *Babylonian and Assyrian Religion*, Oxford, 1962.

Horace, *Odes and Epodes*, Loeb, 1968.

Howell, Alice, *The Dove in the Stone*, London, 1988.

Hyginus, *Fabulae*, Leyden, 1967.

Hyppolytus,*Refutatio*, Edinburgh 1967.

Ions, Veronica, *Egyptian Mythology*, London, 1965.

Irish Catholic Directory and Almanac, Dublin.

Isidoros, *Hymns*.

Jackson, K., *A Celtic Miscellany*, London, 1951.

Jameson, Mrs., *Legends of the Madonna*, London, 1872.

Jonas, H., *The Gnostic Religion*, Boston, 1958.

Josephus, F., 'Antiquities of the Jews' in *Works*, London, 1846.

Joyce, Patrick, *A Social History of Ancient Ireland*, London, 1903.

Julian, the Emperor,*Works*, Loeb.

The Kalevala, London, 1907.

Keating, G., *General History of Ireland*, Dublin, 1859.

Kerenyi, C., *Eleusis*, London, 1967.

_____ *Athene*, Dallas, 1978.

_____ *Goddesses of Sun and Moon*, Dallas, 1979.

King, L., *Babylonian Religion and Mythology*, London, 1899.

Koppana, Catherine, *Manuscript on Finnish Festivals*, 1979.

Kramer, S., *Mythologies of the Ancient World*, New York, 1961,

_____ *The Sacred Marriage Rite*, New York, 1969.

Lady-Unique-Inclination-of-the-Night, Cycles 1-5, New Brunswick, NJ, 1976-80.

Langdon, S., *The Babylonian Epic of Creation*, London, 1923.

_____ *Babylonian Menologies and the Semitic Calendars*, London 1933.

Larson, Martin, *The Religion of the Occident*, London, 1959.

The Lectionary and Alternative Calendars, 1961 and 1981, London, 1981.

Lehner, E. & L., *Folklore and Symbolism of Flowers, Plants and Trees*, New York, 1960.

Lempriere, J., *A Classical Dictionary*, London, 1812.

Levy, G.Rachel, *The Phoenix' Nest*, London, 1961.

Lewis, *Topographical Dictionary of England*.

Libanius, *The Julianic Orations*, Loeb, 1969.

Lucian, *Imagines*, Loeb, 1969.

Lux Madriana, *Calendar of Our Lady's Ekklesia on Earth*, formerly 40 St John Sreet, Oxford.

The Mabinogian, London, 1975.

Macalister, R.A.S., *Tara, a Pagan Sanctuary of Ancient Ireland*, London, 1931.

_____ (trs), *Lebor Gabala Erenn (The Book of Invasions)*, Dublin, 1938.

Mackenzie, W., *The Imperial Dictionary of Universal Biography*, 1863-4.

MacLean, Adam, *The Triple Goddess*, Edinburgh, 1983.

_____ *Four Fire Festivals*.

Marcellinus, Ammianus, *History*, Loeb.

Markale, Jean, *Women of the Celts*, London, 1975.

Maspero, Gaston, *The Dawn of Civilization*, London, 1894.

Massey, Gerald, *The Natural Genesis*, London, 1883.

_____ *Tracts*.

Masters, R., *The Goddess Sekhmet*, Warwick, NY, 1988.

Maternus, Julius Firmicus, *De Errore Profanum Religionum*, Florence, 1969.

Matriarchy News (Journal), Sisterwrite Bookshop, 190 Upper Street, London N1.

McIntosh, *The Religious History of Modern France*.

Mead, G.R.S., *Thrice-Greatest Hermes*, London, 1906.

Montfaucon, Bernard, *Supplement to Antiquity Explained*, c.18C.

Moore, Thomas, *The History of Ireland*, London, 1846.

Mosheim, J.L., *Institutes of Ecclesiastical History*, London, 1841.

Musaeus, *Hero and Leander*, Loeb, 1975.

Musaios, *The Lion Path* (3rd edn), Berkeley, 1988.

Neumann, Erich,*The Great Mother*, London, 1955.

The New Larousse.

Nicholls, Ross, *Manuscript on Celtic Festivals*, c.1970.

Nicholson, Irene, *Mexican and Central American Mythology*, London, 1968.

O'Brien, Henry, *The Round Towers of Ireland*, republished as *Atlantis in Ireland*, New York, 1976.

O'Connor, R., *The Chronicles of Erin*, London, 1822.

Ovid, *The Metamorphoses*, London, 1759.

_____ *Fasti*, Loeb, 1967.

Oxford Classical Dictionary, Oxford.

Pauly-Wissowa (ed), *Real-Encyclopaedia*.

Pausanias, *Travels in Greece*, Harmondsworth, 1980.

Peacock, *Collected Works: Gryll Grange*.

Pereira, E., *Descent to the Goddess*, Toronto, 1981.

Perowne, Stuart, *Roman Mythology*, London, 1969.

Perpetual Festival Calendar, Shrine of Wisdom, Fintry Brook, nr Godalming, Surrey.

Petrie, Wm. Flinders, *Personal Religion in Egypt before Christianity*, London, 1909.

Philocalus, *Kalendarium Antiquum Furii Dionysii Filocali: Anno CCCLIV Conscriptum* in J.Migne, *Patrologia Latina* 13, 1845.

Philostratus,*The Life of Apollonius of Tyana*, Loeb, 1969.

Pinches, T., *The Religion of Babylonia and Assyria*, London, 1906.

Pindar, *Odes*, Loeb, 1968.

Plato, *The Republic*, Harmondsworth, 1971.

Plutarch, *Lives*, London, 1970.

_____ *De Iside et Osiride*, Loeb, 1969.

Porphyry, *The Cave of the Nymphs in the Odyssey*, New York, 1969.

Propertius, *Writings*, Loeb, 1976.

Ptolemy, *Tetrabiblos*, Loeb, 1971.

Ramsey, A., *Les Voyages de Cyrus*, London, 1799.

Rapin de Thoyras, Paul de, *The History of England*, London, 1726-31.

Regardie, I., *The Golden Dawn*, Chicago, 1939.

Richer, Jean, *La Géographie Sacrée du Monde Grec*, Paris, 1964.

Robertson, Olivia, *The Call of Isis*, Clonegal, 1975.

Rolleston, T.W., *Myths and Legends of the Celtic Race*, London, 1911.

Rose, H.J., *A Handbook of Greek Mythology*, London, 1974.

Ross, Anne, *Pagan Celtic Britain*, London & New York, 1968.

Sandars, N.K., *The Epic of Gilgamesh*, Harmondsworth, 1971.

Sappho, *Poems and Fragments*, Ann Arbor, 1965.

Sayce, A., *The Religions of Ancient Egypt and Babylonia*, Edinburgh, 1902.

Seyffert, O., *A Dictionary of Classical Antiquities*, London, 1894.

Shuttle, P. et al., *The Wise Wound*, New York, 1978.

Silvius, *Kalendarium Antiquum Polemei Silvii Anno CCCCIIL Conscriptum* in J.Migne, *Patrologia Latina*, 123, 1845.

Simos, Miriam, *The Spiral Dance: The Rebirth of the Ancient Religion of the Great Goddess*, London, 1979.

Spenser, Edmund, 'The Shepheards Calendar', in *The Complete Works*, London, 1869.

Steiger, Brad, *Gods of Aquarius*, London, 1976.

Stobart, J.C., *The Grandeur that was Rome*, London, 1925.

Stone, Merlin, *The Paradise Papers*, London, 1976.

Temple, Robert, *The Sirius Mystery*, London, 1976.

Tindall, G., *A Handbook of Witches*, London, 1972.

Ulster Journal of Archaeology.

Unicorn Gardens.

Valiente, Doreen, *The ABC of Witchcraft, Past and Present*, London, 1973.

Varro, Marcus, *De Re Rustica*, Loeb, 1979.

Virgil, *Eclogues*, Loeb, 1968.

Waite, A.E., *The Brotherhood of the Rosy Cross*, London, 1924.

Weigall, Arthur, *Wanderings in Roman Britain*, London, 1926.

Whistler, L., *The English Festivals*, London, 1947.

Williams, Athene, *The Story of Isis and Osiris: A Ritual Drama*, Clonegal, 1975.

Wilson, Robert Anton, *The Cosmic Trigger*, London, 1979.

Witt, R.E., *Isis in the Graeco-Roman World*, London, 1971.

Wood, Thomas, *An Inquiry concerning the Primitive Inhabitants of Ireland*, London, 1821.

Yeats, W.B., 'Red Hanrahan' in *Mythologies*, London, 1897.

Young, Jean, *The Prose Edda of Snorri Sturluson*, California, 1971.

Zosimus, *Histoire Nouvelle*.

Special Acknowledgements

Thanks are given to the following publishers for special permission to quote from their productions:

Bear and Co., from *The Illuminations of Hildegard of Bingen* by Matthew Fox (Hildegard of Bingen, 17 September).

Jonathan Cape Ltd, from *The Holy Blood and The Holy Grail* by Baigent, Leigh and Lincoln (Mary Magdalen, 22 July).

Wm. Heinemann Ltd, for quotations from the Loeb Classical Library.

Oxford University Press (see bibliography)

Phanes Press, from *Awakening Osiris*, trs. Normandi Ellis (The Knot of Isis, final pages).

Thames & Hudson Ltd, for quotations from *Isis in the Graeco-Roman World*.

Index